THE GALLAGHER WAY

Arthur J. Gallagher/1892–1985/Founder, Arthur J. Gallagher & Co.

THE
GALLAGHER
WAY

◆

A Corporate History of
Arthur J. Gallagher & Co.

Alison Kittrell

iUniverse, Inc.
Bloomington

The Gallagher Way
A Corporate History of Arthur J. Gallagher & Co.

iUniverse books may be ordered through booksellers or by contacting:

iUniverse
1663 Liberty Drive
Bloomington, IN 47403
www.iuniverse.com
1-800-Authors (1-800-288-4677)

Original layout and design by Wildenradt Design Associateswww.wda25.com

ISBN: 978-0-595-37114-3 (sc)
ISBN: 978-0-595-81514-2 (e)

Printed in the United States of America

iUniverse rev. date: 2/20/2012

Contents

Volume II

Volume I

When *The Gallagher Way* was published in 1996, it told the story of a remarkable company. But the story was far from over, and the pace of the tale picked up considerably. At the end of 1995, Arthur J. Gallagher & Co. had about $412 million in revenues. In 2002, it topped $1 billion in gross revenues and was the third-largest broker in the United States, the fourth-largest in the world. In 2003, its gross revenues rose to $1.3 billion. Still, this world-leading company is clearly the same, in its strategy, culture and values, as the company whose humble beginnings were described in 1996. This book includes two volumes. Volume I is unchanged from the first publication. Volume II tells the rest of the story. At least so far…

Prologue

The story of Arthur J. Gallagher & Co. is, in a very real sense, the story of its people. The people are the engine that drives this company, and each of them is an important part of this story. Only a relatively few people can be mentioned by name, but they represent the contributions and the efforts of all the thousands of Gallagher employees–past, present and future. Arthur J. Gallagher & Co. truly values the commitment of all its people, for this is a company that believes strongly that, "Our most important assets go up and down the elevators every day."

Prologue

Chapter 1
The Immigrant Dream

"Give me your tired, your poor, your huddled masses yearning to breathe free…"

Emma Lazarus, "The New Colossus," plaque on the Statue of Liberty, New York

During the last half of the 19th century, more than 2 million men, women and children fled famine and poverty in Ireland to settle in the United States. Too little is known about most of these travelers, or about immigrants from other countries and in other times. Their individual stories of courage and faith are lost, leaving only the general sense of a country settled by people who were willing to take chances, who believed in themselves, who saw a brighter future and pursued it across oceans and continents. • One of these Irish immigrants was a young boy named John James Gallagher, who became the father of Arthur J. Gallagher. John, who was called Jack, made the journey to America all alone, although he was no more than 10. • Jack probably came to the United States in the 1860s or 1870s. This was years after the great potato famine of the middle and late 1840s, but Ireland was still a very poor country, with little to offer its younger sons. Many of them decided to take their chances in the brave New World. • When Jack said goodbye to his mother in Limerick, Ireland, both of them knew they would never see each other again. In a drama acted out millions of times in all corners of the world, he turned away from his past and sailed off to what he hoped would be a better future. His grandsons later believed that the courage and self-reliance their grandfather had shown in coming to America became an important part of their characters—and of the character of the company that their father went on to establish.

Little is known about the facts of Jack's emigration and his early years in his new country. One version of the story says that young Jack made the trip from Ireland to Boston, then traveled on to Chicago in search of his brother. When he arrived in Chicago, though, the brother had died or moved away. The Irish neighbors took in young Jack, but he missed his mother and wanted to go home, so the neighbors gave him money for the return passage. However, when the boy was standing at the harbor in Boston, ready to board a ship for Ireland, he remembered that he had been seasick all the way over. He decided he didn't want to do that again, and he went back to Chicago.

According to another story, Jack came to live with his brother, who was a police officer in New York. The older brother had left Ireland several years earlier, so when the younger brother walked into the precinct house unannounced, the older brother didn't recognize him. The youngster piped up, "Don't ya know me? I'm John James."

Yet another version is that Jack came to Chicago to live with a cousin who worked in a shoe store on Lake Street. The cousin had written to his relatives in Ireland, telling them of the wonders of his new home, and young Jack decided to see it for himself.

As a young man, Jack became a salesman, beginning a Gallagher tradition of sales. In fact, decades later his grandsons, owners of one of the largest insurance brokerage companies in the world, would refer proudly to themselves as "peddlers."

Jack Gallagher was an impressive salesman, with a certain amount of wanderlust. A photo shows him in Dallas in the 1870s, for example, and he also spent time in Salt Lake City.

His experience in Salt Lake City showed his keen understanding of the importance of knowing your customer. He was selling zithers, and he discovered that it was very hard for an Irish Catholic immigrant to sell zithers to the largely Mormon population of Salt Lake City. So he became a Mormon—and sold a lot of zithers. Later, when he left Salt Lake City, he converted back to Catholicism.

Eventually, Jack Gallagher settled in the large Irish community on the West Side of Chicago. He married Mary Fitzpatrick, a schoolteacher whose ancestors had come from Virginia to Kentucky to Illinois. Jack and Mary became the parents of Gertrude, Daniel, Alice and their youngest child, born on December 23, 1892, whom they named Arthur James.

The West Side neighborhood where the Gallaghers lived centered around St. Columbkille Parish, at 1648 W. Grand. Like most Catholic immigrant neighborhoods, the West Side produced its share of priests. It also was the childhood home of several men who became very influential in the business and sports history of Chicago, including Arthur J. Gallagher, George "Papa Bear" Halas and Jim Hannah, owner of Hannah Trucking Co. and Hannah Inland Waterways and grandfather of actress Daryl Hannah.

But St. Columbkille's Parish and its environs was a very tough neighborhood, the home of Roger "the Terrible" Touhy and his brothers, the sons of an alcoholic Chicago policeman. All of the Touhy boys turned to crime, and all died violently.

The Gallaghers learned early how to stand up for themselves against bullies like the Touhys. One of the Touhy brothers had a long scar across his cheek, courtesy of Gertrude Gallagher. He had tried to steal her ice skates, and she had retaliated by hitting him across the face, slashing him with the blade.

Incidents like these made the Touhys less than anxious to tangle with the Gallaghers. As a young man, Art was returning on the trolley from a date with his future wife, Katherine Madden, who lived on the North Side. He was walking home from the trolley stop under a darkened viaduct when he heard the sound of the distinctive walk of "Tit" Touhy, who had a clubfoot, following him. Tit had been hiding under the viaduct, waiting to relieve some wee-hours stroller of his wallet.

When Art realized that he was being followed–and by whom–he said loudly, "Tit, it's Art Gallagher." Tit came out of the shadows–holding a huge gun. "Art," he said cheerily, "what are you doing out this late?"

Young Art grew up with a passion for sports. He was a gangly kid, thin and wiry with big Irish hands, and he was an excellent pool player. In fact, when he was in his early teens, the family lived upstairs from Kelly's Saloon and Pool Emporium, and Art sometimes played "for the house."

He also was an accomplished bowler. As an adult, he bowled in the Classic League, made up of the best bowlers in the city of Chicago.

But his special love was baseball. As a boy, he got a job cleaning up at the old Chicago Cubs baseball park on the West Side for $5 a week. The job not only gave him an income, but it allowed him to hang out with the ballplayers. He picked up a lot about baseball–and no doubt a fair amount about life–from his new friends, and he developed into an impressive young ballplayer. In fact, he had hopes of signing a professional contract with the Chicago Cubs.

These baseball dreams were unpopular with his parents, Jack and Mary, however. They had higher ambitions for their youngest son than a life spent in the company of ballplayers, whom they felt were a bad influence. So, after his graduation from grammar school, they sent Art to high school.

Art went to DePaul to study bookkeeping. After earning his three-year bookkeeping degree, he started work at the Prussian National Insurance Co., beginning a lifelong relationship with the insurance industry.

About this time, also, he met Katherine Madden. Katherine, the oldest of four children of Patrick and Katherine Garvey Madden, was a schoolteacher.

When Art began dating Katherine, the Maddens were North Side Irish, with a big house, a comfortable income and an elevated social status. The Gallaghers were from "the wrong side of the tracks." The Maddens were uncertain about the future prospects of Art. They liked him personally, and they respected his intelligence and ambition. But, at least in Art's view, they would have preferred that he be of a slightly higher social class.

Patrick Madden came to Chicago from Rochester, New York, where he owned a plumbing supply business that had a huge sign. During a storm, the sign blew down on a man and killed him. This accident so devastated Patrick Madden that he sold his business in Rochester and moved to Chicago.

In Chicago, he became a vice president of James B. Clow and Sons, a plumbing supply house and cast-iron pipe manufacturer on Chicago's West Side. He also was an inventor who developed many innovations in the plumbing industry. He invented the first gravity flushing toilet, and he invented the bubbling water fountain after he saw people coughing with tuberculosis using the public drinking glasses on a train.

He also was a leader in the development of sanitation methods. After disease began to devastate crews working to build the Panama Canal, he was recruited to go to Panama to set up a sanitation system. He also was called to Cuba on a similar mission.

Despite the differences in family status, though, Katherine's affection for Art grew. Soon, however, the young couple's courtship ran into opposition from another, larger source. World War I broke out, and in 1917, Art enlisted in the Army's Illinois 33rd Division, 108th Engineers.

Art was sent to Texas to train, and then went to France to serve under the legendary John J. "Black Jack" Pershing. Art served as a combat engineer in the trenches with his childhood buddy, Eddie Daly, who later became superintendent of detectives in Chicago. According to stories the two told later, they won the war together.

The humorous anecdotes, though, masked the realities of war that the two experienced in France. The 33rd Division saw action in nine major engagements. The division's final count was 798 killed, 7,527 wounded, 18 captured and four missing. Its members went home laden with medals, including 118 awarded by the United States, 52 awarded by England, 47 by France, and one by Belgium. Art's whole battalion was decorated for bravery by the French government. Art, who had risen through the ranks to sergeant major, was notified that he had been selected for officers training just before the armistice of November 11, 1918.

Art came home an officer and a gentleman in 1919. During the war, the Prussian National had been confiscated, so Art went to work for Moore Case Lyman & Hubbard, again as a bookkeeper. At that time there were no major national brokers; insurance was sold by small agents, many of whom also worked at other jobs. Moore Case Lyman & Hubbard was the largest insurance agency in the city, located in the Insurance Exchange building in the Loop.

On April 22, 1920, Art and Katherine Madden were married. Their union would last 65 years, until Art's death in 1985, and produce four children.

Art's love for baseball also continued. He played in semi-professional leagues for many years. His playing days finally ended in the mid-1920s in Three Lakes, Wisconsin.

Art had been asked to play as a ringer in a baseball tournament in Three Lakes. In those days, towns had their own teams, and a lot of betting was done at tournaments such as this one. For his efforts, Art was to be paid $20 a game, or a total of $60–not an insignificant amount of money for a weekend of games.

He was playing third base in a close game, with runners on base. The batter hit a sharp ground ball to Art, who fielded it cleanly and turned to start the double play. The runner coming in from second base had no chance of being safe, so he opted instead to break up the play, coming in spikes high and slamming into Art's knees. The resulting injury ended Art's playing career, and left him with permanent damage to his knees.

Even before the injury, though, baseball was only a passionate diversion. Business became the focus of Art's life. His experience at Moore Case confirmed something that Art had come to realize at Prussian National: The people making the real money in insurance were the people selling it. Arthur J. Gallagher was confident that he could sell insurance, too.

He made a deal with his new employers. If he could get his regular bookkeeping work done, either by coming in early or by staying late, he could try his hand at selling insurance. Moore Case had nothing to lose from the agreement. They got a commission on every piece of business their enterprising young bookkeeper sold, and they got their clerical work done, too. And, since Art was paid on commission, Moore Case only paid him if he made money.

And make money he did. He just went out and rang doorbells, developing the cold-calling expertise that would serve him so well several years later. Soon he was the top producer at Moore Case, and hung up his bookkeeper's pencil forever.

Patrick Madden had died while Art was in France. Madden was a dandy, changing his suits several times a day, and he also was a generous man. Every day when he got off the train, panhandlers were waiting for him because they knew he would drop a quarter in their cups—a princely sum in those days.

One of these panhandlers made Patrick Madden his heir, and when the man died, he left some property in a place called Smackover, Arkansas. Years later the property turned out to be in the middle of an oil field, and Art Gallagher went to Smackover and negotiated a lucrative mineral rights agreement. Katherine Garvey Madden rewarded her son-in-law for his negotiating skills with a pat on the back and some used furniture.

By this time, Art and Katherine were living in Hubbard Woods, in the northern suburbs of Chicago, with their growing family. They welcomed all four of their children during the 1920s: A. James (Jim) on July 9, 1921; Robert E. (Bob) on January 1, 1923; Katherine (Kate) on December 11, 1925; and John P. on August 9, 1927.

The family grew, and Art continued to sell insurance. But he increasingly was troubled by the realization that he was seen at the agency as its only "street guy," while the rest of the producers were perceived as having higher social status, being more upscale. The final straw came when he discovered that, despite his position as top producer, he was being paid less than the "fancy Dans."

Art was outraged. He was the best salesman the agency had, and he was not being compensated for that. He had developed a close working and personal relationship with the Hartford Accident and Indemnity insurance company and George H. Maloney Sr., who headed the Chicago office of Hartford A&I. So, with the blessing of Maloney and with Hartford A&I as his first insurer, Arthur J. Gallagher wrote the following letter, and Arthur J. Gallagher & Co. was born:

August 25, 1927.

Moore Case Lyman & Hubbard,
Insurance Exchange,
Chicago Ill.,

        Attention of Mr. F. W. Moore,
        Personal & Confidential.

Gentlemen:

        After due consideration, I wish to terminate
my association with the firm of Moore Case Lyman &
Hubbard, my resignation to take effect October 1, 1927.

                Yours very truly,

Chapter 2
The Birth Of A Company

"The future never just happened. It was created."

Will and Ariel Durant

Arthur J. Gallagher put a lot on the line when he left his position with Moore Case Lyman & Hubbard to start his own company. As a young husband and father with four children, he had many responsibilities. But he also had a lot of confidence. He was angry about the way he had been treated at Moore Case, and he was certain that he could do better on his own. • He was not without contacts, of course. He started Arthur J. Gallagher & Co. with the blessing of George H. Maloney Sr., head of the Chicago office of the Hartford Accident and Indemnity insurance company. Virtually all of the liability and workers compensation business of the young agency was placed through Hartford A&I. However, all the Chicago assignments for the Hartford were being used at the time Art started his business, so for a while, the business of the young agency was "bootlegged" through Minneapolis. The agency's property placements were through a subsidiary of the Home Insurance Co. • Most of the business of Arthur J. Gallagher & Co. resulted from Art's persistent knocking on doors. Art decided at the start that he was going to concentrate on commercial insurance rather than personal lines. Commercial accounts had been his specialty at Moore Case, and he knew that was where the real money was.

Art was a tremendous cold caller. One of his friends said years later that, "He had a thick pair of soles and a ball-bearing tongue." He was an exceptionally persuasive salesman once he got his foot in the door, and he was extremely persistent.

Once, early in his career, Art called on a business. He had no appointment, but he gave his card to the receptionist and asked her to give it to the owner and inquire as to whether Art could talk with him about his insurance coverage.

Through the open office door, he saw the receptionist take the card to the owner, and then he saw the owner tear up the card and throw it away. The receptionist came back out and told Art that the owner was too busy to talk to him.

Art said he understood and asked for his card back. The receptionist, flustered, re-entered the office and told the owner, "Mr. Gallagher wants his card back." The owner, now annoyed, gave the receptionist a nickel. Following the owner's instruction, the receptionist told Art she had lost his card, and gave him a nickel to pay for it.

Art dug into his pocket and, putting another card on the table, said to the receptionist, "Give this card to your boss, and tell him they're two for a nickel."

Persistence was only one of the founding characteristics of Arthur J. Gallagher & Co. Art also understood the importance of being close to the markets. His relationship with Maloney and Hartford A&I was vital to the survival and growth of Arthur J. Gallagher & Co., and not only because it provided the young agency with a willing market. Maloney was a friend and confidant of Art, acting as a sounding board and adviser. One of the most valuable pieces of advice Maloney gave, however, was not about business.

Maloney told Art there was a young woman in the Kansas City office of Hartford A&I who was a native of Chicago and wanted desperately to come home. She was an excellent worker and a fine person, Maloney said, and she would be invaluable to Art and his new company.

So, at Maloney's suggestion, Art hired the homesick young woman from Kansas City in 1928. She was Mabel Pottinger, and she became one of the most important employees of Arthur J. Gallagher & Co. She helped shape the company, she helped train succeeding generations of company leaders, including Jim, Bob and John Gallagher, and later Patrick Gallagher, and she left an indelible mark on the company she served for 44 years, until her retirement in 1972.

In addition to knowing his markets, Art believed in knowing his customers. He realized that there were lots of insurance agents, and businesses could buy coverage anywhere. They even could buy comparable coverage at a comparable price. So he determined that he would provide the kind of service that would keep his customers happy, and keep them coming back. Arthur J. Gallagher & Co. has continued this tradition and, as a result, always has enjoyed exceptional loyalty from its customers.

Many of Art's customers also became social acquaintances and friends. In addition to his childhood friends Jim Hannah and George Halas, legendary owner of the Chicago Bears, Art and Katherine counted as clients and friends Francis and Betty Kullman of Bowman Dairy; the Rasmussen family, owners of the National Tea Co.; the Morris family, with a number of interests related to the Chicago Stockyards; and other notable Chicagoans.

James B. Clow, owner of the plumbing supply business where Patrick Madden had been a vice president, became a special mentor to Art Gallagher. For years, Art treasured a letter from James B. Clow offering the young entrepreneur some business advice. The theme of the letter–a message Art took to heart–was that a business could easily be ruined if the top man developed too big an ego and too strong a hunger for power.

Rather than seeking power for himself, Art looked for ways to put power into the hands of his clients. Arthur J. Gallagher & Co. developed concepts of risk management before there was such a term. At the time, companies thought little about ways to reduce their losses. Insurance was readily available and reasonably priced, and there was an ample labor pool. There was little financial incentive for businesses to worry about risk management.

But Art believed that businesses could find ways to reduce their losses, and in the process could realize significant savings of money, time, productivity, and even lives. He began to work with his clients to identify areas of risk and to develop and implement ways to reduce that risk.

For example, he developed a system of rewards and penalties for truck drivers. In addition to Hannah Trucking, Art's clients included dairies and other businesses that transported goods, making truck safety a natural focus. According to the system he pioneered, truck drivers received financial incentives for driving safely, and were penalized for chargeable accidents or other unsafe driving. This system is common now—trucks routinely have a toll-free number painted on them urging motorists to call with complaints or compliments. But at the time, it was revolutionary.

And it was effective. Years later, Bob Gallagher remembered several times when, as a young boy driving with his father, a trucker would drive recklessly past them. Then the trucker, recognizing the elder Gallagher's car, would roll down his window and yell, "Sorry, Art."

This emphasis on risk management—on reducing both the financial and the human cost of risk—would become a cornerstone of Arthur J. Gallagher & Co. and Gallagher Bassett, as they helped to create the universe of self-insurance and alternative markets.

In the late 1920s, though, Arthur J. Gallagher & Co. was really only Arthur J. Gallagher and a secretary—and, after 1928, Mabel Pottinger. Then, on October 29, 1929, the New York Stock Exchange crashed; stock losses reached an estimated $50 billion by 1931.

Millionaires became paupers. Bank failures and suicides were common. Businesses folded and farmers lost their land. By 1932, unemployment nationwide was running 25 percent, and the homeless had set up "Hoovervilles" in major cities.

Chicago was hit hard by the Great Depression, and it became hard to sell commercial insurance in a period of business failures. But Art Gallagher kept knocking on doors, persuading business owners that it was especially critical in uncertain financial times that they protect what they had. He promised himself that he would increase his pay every month during the Depression. And, despite overwhelming odds, he kept his promise.

In fact, by the mid-1930s, the business of Arthur J. Gallagher & Co. was becoming too great for Art to handle, even with Mabel's assistance. Art had been impressed by an enterprising neighbor of his in Hubbard Woods, and he made one of the most important cold calls of his life on that neighbor, Dan Wachs. As a boy, Dan had mowed the Gallaghers' grass and sometimes caddied for Art; he remembered that Art tipped 50 cents rather than the usual 25 cents. So, when Art came calling, Dan agreed to take a position with Arthur J. Gallagher & Co.

Dan was joined a few years later by Ed Keating. Ed was married to the youngest sister of Francis Kullman of Bowman Dairy, and this relationship was a primary reason that Art hired Ed in the first place. However, Ed's value to Arthur J. Gallagher & Co. grew to be much more than the Bowman Dairy account.

At first, Dan and Ed provided technical support for Art's sales. They dealt with the insurance companies and drew up the technical paperwork related to the policies, while Art made the sales.

This arrangement reflected a harsh reality: One of the biggest threats to an agent's business was other agents in his office. Most agencies, therefore, were set up along the lines of Arthur J. Gallagher & Co., with principals acting as salesmen and the rest of the staff providing the technical support. This gave the salesmen more time to sell, and it reduced the risk of employees making off with the customers.

At Arthur J. Gallagher & Co., though, an evolution began that would prove to be one of the defining characteristics of the company: a sales staff that knew both the technical and the sales sides of the business. Dan and Ed gradually became more than technicians. As the business grew, they took over the servicing of some of Art's existing accounts. Eventually, they became important producers in their own right.

They later would be joined by Art's sons, who were beginning to learn the business. During the prewar years, Jim and Bob often worked in the Insurance Exchange office of Arthur J. Gallagher & Co. They ran errands, did odd jobs, and generally acted as "go-fers." Decades later, sitting at his desk as chairman of Arthur J. Gallagher & Co., Bob Gallagher remembered the fun of those summers, when he started on the switchboard for $5 a week and moved up to messenger.

"We got to watch my dad and Dan and Ed, and I loved it," he said. "I was always enthusiastic and ambitious about the business, even in those days. Other boys who were working as messengers in the building would take the elevator, but I always ran up the stairs. I couldn't stand to wait for the elevator."

It was exciting for Bob and Jim to go downtown, to work at the "family store," to have jobs to do. Like the children of many self-employed people, they were used to hearing the business discussed at their dinner table. The financial rhythm of their lives depended on what was now referred to as AJGCo.: A big sale or renewal was cause for celebration, while the rare lost account brought a tightening of the belt. Their experience at the office gave them a greater under-standing of the business that their father was building.

Bob and Jim also discovered during those summers, working under the watch-ful tutelage of Mabel Pottinger, that they liked the business of insurance. They liked the excitement and the personal contact of sales. They enjoyed watching Art, Dan and Ed in action. They began to think of the company and their futures as inexorably intertwined.

These were exciting days for AJGCo. as well. The company showed its groundbreaking capacity early when, in the spring of 1938, Arthur J. Gallagher & Co. helped to create the Retrospective Rating Program of the Hartford Group. The program was so innovative that the paperwork for the first retro policy the agency wrote was kept in Dan Wachs' bottom drawer until the program became legal in the state of Illinois.

Retro rating, which gave customers credit for holding down their losses, was a first step toward self-insurance and the alternative market. With its emphasis on providing financial incentives for reducing losses, the coverage presaged the development of risk management services.

AJGCo. took another major step toward the world of self-insurance when it wrote the first large-deductible fire policy in Chicago, for Bowman Dairy Co. Large deductibles and experience rating are common now; in fact, they seem almost outdated today. But in the late 1930s, they became the first rumblings of a revolution that would sweep the insurance industry. And Arthur J. Gallagher & Co. would be on the front lines of that revolution.

During the '30s, AJGCo. continued its close relationship with insurers, break-ing new ground in cooperation between agents and carriers. Representing Hart-ford for casualty coverage and the Home Insurance Co. for fire policies, AJGCo. was authorized to issue binders and to type and sign its own policies.

Insurers provided such freedom to AJGCo. because they had come to trust Art and his agency. They admired his integrity and his innovation in the service of his clients and his carriers, and they were willing to join their fortunes with his.

Chapter 3
The Next Generation

"The toughest thing about success is that you've got to keep on being a success."

Irving Berlin

During the 1930s in Chicago, the business of Arthur J. Gallagher & Co. was growing. Art, Dan Wachs and Ed Keating were selling insurance at a fine clip. Bob and Jim Gallagher were growing up, working summers at the office and eventually heading to college. John Gallagher was beginning to take his turn working under Mabel's watchful eye. The country was battling its way out of the Depression. • But abroad, a cancer was growing. The Nazi Party, under the direction of Adolph Hitler, came to power in Germany in 1933. Fascism began to spread across the continent of Europe. General Francisco Franco triumphed in the Spanish Civil War, and the Nazis took over Austria and most of Czechoslovakia without opposition. • On September 1, 1939, the German army marched into Poland, and Great Britain and France no longer could look the other way; both countries declared war on Hitler's Germany. In 1940, Italy, under Benito Mussolini, entered the war on Germany's side. In June 1940, France fell to the Axis powers. • Although the United States was not yet involved directly in the war, the conflict had captured the thoughts of the nation. A fierce debate was taking place about how long the country could continue to remain outside the fray.

Then, on December 7, 1941–"a day that will live in infamy"–the Japanese bombed the U.S. fleet stationed at Pearl Harbor, Hawaii. More than 2,000 Americans were killed, and about 1,000 were injured. All eight battleships of the U.S. Pacific fleet were damaged, and three were destroyed. The U.S.S. Arizona was sunk in the harbor, taking 1,102 sailors with her to their deaths. A stunned United States declared war on Japan, Germany and Italy.

Jim Gallagher and Bob Gallagher were in college at Cornell University in Ithaca, New York. Over Christmas 1941, both Gallagher sons enlisted in Naval Aviation.

Jim was a junior at Cornell and Bob was a sophomore. Jim was called up in the summer of 1942. He received his wings in early 1943, and served in the South Pacific in Naval Air Transport.

Bob was called up a year later. He received his wings in late 1944 and qualified as a carrier dive bomber pilot. After graduating from high school in 1945, John Gallagher followed his brothers into the Navy, serving on a seaplane tender in the South Pacific.

Dan Wachs also joined the service during the war. Then, in 1944, Art Gallagher became gravely ill with rheumatic fever. Bob was called back from flight training to see his father, who had shrunk to 90 pounds and was not expected to live.

While Jim, Bob, John and Dan were in service and Art was fighting for his life in Florida, where he had gone to recover from the rheumatic fever, the business of Arthur J. Gallagher & Co. was kept alive by Mabel Pottinger and Ed Keating, who was medically ineligible for service. Miraculously, they managed not only to retain the existing business, but also to add new accounts.

Perhaps as important, they demonstrated a loyalty to the business that has become a hallmark of the employees of Arthur J. Gallagher & Co. The great fear of any insurance agency–piracy–was not realized. Although the company's founder was recovering in Florida and his sons were serving in the Navy, Ed and Mabel did not make off with any business themselves, and they fiercely defended the agency's business against outside raiders. Somehow, against great odds, they managed to hold the company together until the end of the war.

After the war, a new chapter in the history of Arthur J. Gallagher & Co. began. Among the legions of young men coming back from battle and joining the work force were the sons of Art and Katherine Gallagher.

Jim Gallagher joined AJGCo. in 1946. When he left the Navy as a lieutenant, he had been earning the "princely income" of $375 or $400 a month. He started at AJGCo. for $175 a month. And, he said, "I had no business making that, based on what I knew about selling insurance." But he–and his brothers–learned quickly.

Bob returned to finish up as a history and speech major at Cornell. He was very active on campus, as the captain of the basketball team, president of Psi Upsilon fraternity, and a member of honor societies and other organizations. After graduation, he, too, concluded that his future was with "the family store."

John Gallagher, now a student at Cornell himself, had decided that there already were enough Gallaghers at AJGCo., and that the company could not support yet another son. Instead, he decided to be an advertising copywriter, showing an early affinity for marketing.

At a holiday dinner during John's senior year of college, though, Jim and Bob cornered their younger brother and persuaded him to try selling insurance "just for a year." When he graduated from Cornell in 1950, John agreed to try the business for a year–and that year grew to a lifetime.

Although he had survived his bout with rheumatic fever, Arthur J. Gallagher continued to spend much of his time in Florida. In 1950, after John joined the company, Art decided it was time to incorporate the business and include his sons in an official way. The company recorded $175,000 in revenues in 1950, and the original capitalization of Arthur J. Gallagher & Co. was $10,000. Each of the sons received 20 percent of the company, and Art retained 40 percent.

"That way all three of us would have to agree in order to outvote him," Bob Gallagher said. "And he figured he could get at least one of his sons to side with him."

The office to which the Gallagher sons returned after the war consisted of one big office and a "pit" in the Insurance Exchange building. There was one electronic calculator, and a couple of adding machines. All the machines were purchased secondhand, from the Hartford A&I.

Mabel ran the office with an iron fist. She had developed a filing system, for example, based entirely on renewal dates. For any insurance agency, it is critical to be aware of when a policy renews, and Mabel made a folder for every policy the agency wrote and filed them all in chronological order, by renewal date.

Mabel's system was very efficient for remembering renewals; the agency never missed a renewal date. However, the system had some major drawbacks.

For example, every individual policy had its own file folder. But there was no easy way to get a quick picture of a client's total insurance program. The only way to find each policy a client had was to go through the whole system, date by date, looking for the individual policies issued to that client.

Obviously this was an unwieldy system, but its reliance on the all-important renewal dates reflected the fact that the office of Arthur J. Gallagher & Co. was focused on renewing existing accounts and selling new accounts.

It also reflected the power of Mabel Pottinger. As the longest-term employee of Arthur J. Gallagher & Co. and one of the two people responsible for the survival of the business during the war years, Mabel saw the office functions of AJGCo. as her domain, and she was not reluctant to exert her influence.

In fact, years later, in about 1963, Bob Gallagher set up a Suggestion Box, seeking employee input on how to run the office. He offered a first prize of $100, second prize of $50, and third prize of $25. Mabel turned in five single-spaced pages of suggestions; she got third prize for effort.

In addition to the filing idiosyncrasies, the company also did not produce interim financial results. Every year in early December, Mabel did a preliminary financial report. Then, at the end of the year, an accountant came in and did an official profit and loss statement. But there was no real way of knowing where things stood during the year.

The Gallagher sons, especially Jim, wanted to change some of these things. Jim was an early proponent of professional management techniques; he attended classes given by the American Management Association, and he persuaded Bob and John to go, too. But bringing management principles to AJGCo. was not an easy task.

First of all, there was little time for considering how best to run the business; everyone was too busy actually running it. Even with the addition of three new producers in Jim, Bob and John, the selling of new policies and the servicing of existing ones took up all of everyone's time.

"Jim would talk about changes like this, and John and I would just look at him and say, 'Don't worry about this; just go out there and sell insurance,'" Bob remembered.

The push for change also ran into opposition from Mabel, who believed fully in the system she had developed, and from Art, who did not understand why the company needed to go to the trouble of preparing interim financials.

But gradually, change occurred. And in the mid-1950s, the company made a major leap, into the dawning computer age.

Jim was involved in some charitable work for the Red Cross, and among the other businesspeople serving on the Red Cross committee was a man named Mike Natarro, a social acquaintance of the Gallaghers who ran a firm called Statistical Tabulating Company. A major client base for Statistical Tabulating was insurance agencies; the company used computers to generate financial statements and reports to insurance carriers.

Jim Gallagher and Mike Natarro began to talk to each other about their businesses, and Jim was intrigued by the thought of what Natarro's company could do for AJGCo. At about the time Jim was mulling over these conversations, there was a national presidential election. For the first time, computers were used to tabulate returns. Jim, watching at home, was astonished by the speed with which the election results were available, and he came to believe even more strongly in the future of this new technology.

AJGCo. hired Statistical Tabulating to generate its financial reports and its reports to carriers. This move into the computer age became increasingly significant a few years later, in 1957, when the agency got its biggest client yet: Beatrice Foods Co.

Bob Gallagher is fond of saying that his company is "divinely inspired," and the landing of the Beatrice account would seem to bear him out.

Beatrice Foods, even in the mid-1950s, was a major corporation, making significant acquisitions. One of its acquisitions was Blue Valley Creamery, which employed a woman named Edna Merchant. Before going to Blue Valley, Edna Merchant had worked at AJGCo. and, like so many Gallagher employees before and since, she retained a great deal of respect for and loyalty to the Gallaghers. She discovered that Beatrice, the new parent of Blue Valley, was interested in shopping around its insurance coverage, which was brokered by giant Marsh &

McLennan. She decided this information might interest her former employers, so she alerted them.

Arthur J. Gallagher & Co., which was still a relatively small, local agency, decided to go up against the giant M&M. They put together a retro policy through the Travelers and offered it to Beatrice.

Their proposal fell on friendly ears. The insurance manager at Beatrice, Jim Cullen, was a good friend of Art's. They shared a passion for the ponies, and used to go to the racetrack together. Cullen was more than willing to listen to an offer from his friend, whom he knew to be a smart and honest businessman. The AJGCo. bid was far superior to M&M's arrangement and, to the surprise of the larger broker, Beatrice went with Gallagher.

Landing Beatrice put AJGCo. immediately into the big time. It was by far the company's largest account, and it was growing. The relationship between Beatrice and Arthur J. Gallagher & Co. would continue until Beatrice eventually broke up, and it would be the catalyst for a revolution for both Gallagher and the insurance industry.

Chapter 4
With You Or Without You

"They say you can't do it, but sometimes it doesn't always work."

Casey Stengel

The relationship between Beatrice Foods Co. and Arthur J. Gallagher & Co. blossomed rapidly after AJGCo. got the Beatrice account in 1957. Ed Keating handled the casualty side of the account, and Dan Wachs handled the property side. The Gallagher people were part of the Beatrice family. • When they took over the business from Marsh & McLennan, Gallagher put together a state-of-the-art insurance program for Beatrice. But, only a few years later, Beatrice CEO Bill Karnes decided he wanted more control over his costs. He discussed this with the Gallaghers, suggesting that Beatrice might want to buy its own insurance company. • The Gallaghers discouraged him in that idea, pointing out that it would require Beatrice to insure other companies as well as itself and to deal with the myriad regulations that governed insurance companies. OK, Karnes said; then what about self-insurance? • It was a tribute to the relationship between Beatrice and Gallagher that Karnes turned to the Gallaghers for help and counsel. At the same time, it was a serious blow for a brokerage firm to have its largest client talk about leaving the traditional insurance market. But Karnes was adamant, finally telling his broker, "We're doing this with you or without you."

So the Gallaghers began to investigate ways to help Beatrice achieve its goal. At the time, some companies self-insured their workers compensation exposure, obtaining excess coverage through Lloyd's of London. But there was virtually no other commercial self-insurance, no alternative market that could be tapped. If Beatrice was determined to take control of its coverage, then AJGCo. would have to create the mechanism to do that.

The Gallaghers realized that one of the secrets to successful self-insurance would be setting up a claims system. But they were brokers, and, although they all had gone through the insurance training at the Hartford, their area of expertise was placing coverage, not handling claims. They knew that they would have to find someone to help them.

They found that someone in Sterling Bassett. Sterling had spent more than 20 years as a claims adjuster for Western Adjustment Co., which later merged with and became the General Adjustment Bureau. Sterling was a well-respected adjuster, and GAB's top management man in Chicago.

Sterling and Jim Gallagher were neighbors in Park Ridge, and Sterling had come to know Jim and the other brothers socially. Jim and Sterling rode the train into Chicago together every day, and Beatrice's plan became their main topic of discussion. The idea was intriguing to Sterling, but his interest was still strictly intellectual. He had spent his professional lifetime as an adjuster, and it was fascinating to consider how he would set up a system for handling claims if he were in charge. But he had no intention of actually joining the Gallaghers in their unusual new endeavor.

Then Sterling, the Gallagher brothers and Ed Keating gathered for a "boys weekend" at Dairyman's Country Club in Boulder Junction, Wisconsin. They continued their discussions about how to structure a program for Beatrice. Sitting on the dock one night, Sterling said, "If you do decide to do this, who would you get to help you with the claims?" Jim and John Gallagher replied, "What about you?" Then Sterling said, "What would you call this company?" The Gallaghers said, "How about Gallagher Bassett?" No deal was struck but, as John recalled later, "We got Sterling just a little bit pregnant."

During that weekend at Dairyman's, Sterling broke his foot, which laid him up at home for several weeks. Jim Gallagher stopped in almost every night, ostensibly to visit with his convalescing friend, but also to talk about Beatrice.

"Sitting there at home, not working, talking to Jim, I became very deeply mentally involved in this project," Sterling said. He knew that any successful self-insurance effort would have to include a major emphasis on efficient claims handling. In his years of experience, he had observed that insurance companies too often considered adjustments an expense and a nuisance. But Sterling knew that a good adjuster could save significant amounts of money. He knew, for example, that quick action by a fire adjuster to remove water-soaked carpeting could help save the wood floor underneath. A self-insured client, he reasoned, would be more open to the value of adjusting, because that client would be picking up the tab for the losses; any money the adjuster could save would be money the client could keep.

Beatrice would be an ideal candidate for a self-insured program, Sterling thought, because the company had an excellent spread of risk, and its management obviously was committed to the concept.

Still, when the Gallaghers asked Sterling for a list of adjusters who might help them with the Beatrice program, Sterling did not include himself on that list. He had "platinum handcuffs"–a pension from his years of service at GAB–and he was not yet willing to give that up.

Then, a series of events occurred that made Sterling another believer in Bob Gallagher's theory that AJGCo. is "divinely inspired."

First, GAB decided to consolidate its headquarters in New York. Sterling knew he would have to move East if he wanted to continue to advance in his career, but he had no interest in relocating. So he began to consider the Gallagher proposal more seriously.

He knew, though, that he would need help. He played golf with a man named Guenther Ahlf, who was a claims attorney with Allstate. Ahlf's specialty was casualty claims, and Sterling's was property, so they were a good match. And Ahlf could provide the legal expertise that Sterling needed.

Sterling approached Ahlf about the idea, and at first Ahlf was lukewarm. After all, Allstate was an established company and Ahlf had 13 years in there. But he recently had been transferred to Indianapolis, and he badly wanted to get back to Chicago.

Ahlf talked the matter over with his wife, Betty. She was opposed to the move. She didn't like Indianapolis either, but she was not enthusiastic about turning their family fortunes over to one of her husband's golf buddies.

The more she thought about it, though, the more the name of Sterling Bassett seemed familiar to her. Then she remembered: One of her brothers had gone to high school in Glen Ellyn with Sterling. The Bassetts were well-thought-of, she recalled, and so maybe it was worth taking a chance.

Ahlf then took the question to a lawyer friend of his named Allen Greene. At first Greene agreed with Betty Ahlf, that the deal was just too risky, even if it meant coming back to Chicago. Then he, too, remembered that he knew Sterling Bassett.

When Sterling and his wife, Hope, were first married, they lived in an apartment in LaSalle, Illinois. A family named the Greenes lived in the apartment behind them, and they had a son who played basketball on the high school team. Like most high school boys, the Greene boy was always hungry, and Hope Bassett found him a willing taste tester for all her new recipes. The Greenes and the Bassetts moved apart, and years later, Allen Greene—the basketball player who had grown into a lawyer—was surprised to hear a familiar name. He told Ahlf, "I don't know much about this deal, but if that is the Sterling Bassett who is married to Hope, then you take that job."

It was, of course, the Sterling Bassett who was married to Hope, and Ahlf decided to take the job. When Ahlf agreed to join the team, the last piece of the puzzle was in place. Sterling gave his notice at General Adjustment and, on November 10, 1962, Gallagher Bassett was formed.

Beatrice wanted to implement its self-insurance program on March 1, 1963, so there was no time to waste. Sterling, Ed Keating and Jim Cullen, Beatrice's insurance manager, visited all the Beatrice locations around the country to explain to them about the program and to get them involved.

The GB team also had to set up the program, which was, in essence, much like creating an insurance company from scratch. Ahlf and Sterling used their extensive contacts in the adjustment community to set up a network of adjusters around the country. Ahlf drew up claims forms and found attorneys to handle litigation.

Ed Keating and Sterling also scrambled to meet the demands of insurance regulators, who were suspicious of this new idea. There were many hurdles–some of which were expected, and some of which took them by surprise.

For example, certain states, including Massachusetts, required companies to provide proof of liability coverage for truck drivers. Since there was no traditional insurance, there was no such proof.

Good salesmen, though, believe that every obstacle is really just an opportunity in disguise, and this was the opportunity to develop what has become an insurance industry standard: the fronting company. Ed Keating located an insurance company in Texas that would front the coverage, meaning it would write a liability policy–with a side agreement that no claim ever would be filed. This satisfied the requirements of the regulators.

Most of the difficulties Gallagher Bassett encountered with insurance regulators were in the area of workers compensation. Different states had different requirements for workers compensation coverage, and on several occasions, political disputes added to the problem.

Sterling kept at it, though, because he believed that it was critical to get the Beatrice program approved in all the states. His persistence not only made the program possible in those states where Beatrice operated, but it also helped build very important relationships with state insurance regulators–relationships that served the company well as it expanded.

"We ran into many surprises, but we found ways to solve them all," Sterling recalled. "Although the idea was new and different, it was an idea whose time had come."

The traditional insurance industry was distrustful of and even hostile toward Gallagher Bassett, although the industry had been edging in the direction of self-insurance for years, with the development of experience rating and retro policies. Self-insurance went a step further, though, and it was a step that bypassed traditional insurers and brokers. Arthur J. Gallagher & Co. and Gallagher Bassett became very unpopular in the industry.

The Gallaghers believed, though, that self-insurance presented a huge opportunity for brokers like themselves who were willing and able to embrace it. The opportunity would come as companies began to realize the significant advantages of creating and controlling their own risk-protection programs.

Self-insurance gave a client much greater control over its money. Under traditional insurance, the client paid its premiums before there were claims. But with self-insurance, no money was paid until a claim was settled. Claims might not be settled for months or even years; in the meantime, the client got to keep its money.

Self-insurance also provided a strong financial incentive to control losses. With a traditional program, a client paid premiums based on the exposure to loss, whether or not there actually were any losses. With the introduction of experience rating and retro policies, insurers were moving toward giving policyholders some reward for keeping their losses down, but self-insurance made it clear: If a client cut its losses, it got to keep the savings.

Beatrice was especially enthusiastic about this aspect of its new program. The company already had implemented an incentive program for its profit center managers under the old retro policy. Profit centers were charged for their share of the premium and, if their losses were kept low, they got part of the refund. The company called it the "13th-month profit."

Key to realizing this profit, of course, was loss control. Under traditional insurance, there was no particular reason for companies to practice loss control; their insurer simply paid claims when they were incurred. But with self-insurance, there was a big reason for companies to look at risk management issues: Losses were paid right out of the company's pocket.

After a hectic four months, the framework for the Beatrice program was in place. On March 1, 1963–right on schedule–Beatrice became self-insured, changing forever both Arthur J. Gallagher & Co. and the landscape of commercial insurance.

In the months before the Beatrice launch and the months right after, the Gallaghers and Sterling Bassett made several decisions that had significant impact on the course of Gallagher Bassett.

Continuing Art Gallagher's tradition of being close to the client, Gallagher Bassett came to rely heavily on personal contact. It became obvious that the visits by Sterling and Ed Keating to the individual Beatrice locations had helped ease the transition, and Sterling continued that policy. Each time Beatrice acquired a new company, Sterling visited that location to explain the program, to evaluate the location's exposure, and to gain the support of the managers.

"The people at the locations were always very impressed to be visited by the Sterling Bassett of Gallagher Bassett," John Gallagher recalled, laughing. "They didn't realize that, in those days, there was only Sterling Bassett at Gallagher Bassett."

That is a slight exaggeration, of course, but in the beginning, the Gallagher Bassett staff was only Sterling, Guenther Ahlf and Ella Droese, Sterling's secretary. Ella had worked for AJGCo. before moving over to Gallagher Bassett, and she was invaluable in getting the new entity off the ground.

In order to minimize expenses, Sterling and the Gallaghers decided, in effect, not to spend money until they had money. They didn't open an office in a city, for example, unless Beatrice had a location there.

However, Beatrice and GB agreed that there should be a Gallagher Bassett office in virtually every location where there was a Beatrice operation. That meant that when Beatrice acquired a company, Gallagher Bassett had to open an office on the run. Sterling called often on his national network of friends in the adjusting industry to staff those offices.

Sterling and the Gallaghers also decided not to set up an independent sales force for Gallagher Bassett. Instead, Gallagher Bassett would be captive to the sales force of Arthur J. Gallagher & Co. Sterling and Bob Gallagher, who became president and CEO of AJGCo. in 1963, felt this relationship benefited both the sales force and GB. Gallagher Bassett was an attractive product for the brokers, and the brokers could carry the Gallagher Bassett message.

However, the original deal called for Gallagher Bassett to be 50 percent owned by AJGCo. and 50 percent owned by Sterling. Bob realized that, under this arrangement, AJGCo. would not be able to pay a sales force that would allow Gallagher Bassett to grow, and he took his concern to Sterling.

"Sterling understood this and he became an employee like all the rest of us, in a heartbeat," Bob said. The agreement was redrawn, and GB remained captive to the Gallagher brokers for more than 20 years.

During that time, its value to AJGCo. and to its clients continued to grow. Starting with Beatrice, Arthur J. Gallagher & Co. and Gallagher Bassett began to carve out a niche as major suppliers to—and significant developers of—the alternative market.

Self-insurance was a natural extension of the Gallagher philosophy; after all, this was the company that had pioneered the large-deductible fire policy and the retro policy. Arthur J. Gallagher & Co. always has been a leader rather than a follower, believing in the rule that, "It is better to shift than to be shifted." With the establishment of Gallagher Bassett, AJGCo. shifted in a big way, and took the industry with it.

Chapter 5
The Lord's Work

"Change is the law of life. And those who look only to the past or present are certain to miss the future."

President John F. Kennedy

It was 2:40 p.m. on December 1, 1958. The children at Our Lady of the Angels Catholic school at 909 N. Avers in Chicago were thinking about the end of the schoolday at 3 p.m., and about the coming of Christmas at the end of the month. It was a typical Monday–until fire swept up the stairwell. • In an instant, the school turned into a smoke-filled inferno. Multiple fire alarms were sounded, and within moments, firemen, children and nuns filled the street. Soon they were joined by hysterical parents who pushed against the police lines, desperate to find their missing children. These parents were hoping against hope that their child would be among the lucky ones, huddled coughing with their teachers, and not among the grim procession of tiny, limp bodies that sobbing firefighters began to carry out of the school. • Ninety-five people, almost all of them children between 8 and 14, eventually died in the fire. Scores of other children suffered injuries, many of them permanent. The newly arrived archbishop of Chicago, Albert G. Meyer, led the prayers and mourning. • At the direction of Archbishop Meyer, who became cardinal, the archdiocese tribunal adjudicated every claim from the fire. Losses eventually came to $3 million. The archdiocese was woefully underinsured, with only $100,000 in liability coverage on the parish.

Bishop Cletus O'Donnell, who later became bishop of Madison, Wisconsin, and at the time was an official in the chancery office, was a close friend of the Gallaghers. A few years after the Our Lady of the Angels fire, at Bishop O'Donnell's request, Bob Gallagher, John Gallagher, Ed Keating and Dan Wachs put together a $10 million umbrella policy–with broader terms and 10 times the limits of the existing $1 million following form policy–that cost half what the diocese was paying. They invited O'Donnell and Jo Klupar, the archdiocese's business manager, to the AJGCo. offices.

O'Donnell looked at the proposal Bob placed before him, astonished at the broader coverage and the savings. Then he looked up and said softly, "My God, Bob, this would make you cry."

This led to an AJGCo. proposal for an all-lines protected self-insurance plan for the archdiocese. The Gallaghers knew that the archdiocese was a natural candidate for self-insurance. First of all, its existing coverage was inadequate, as the tragic fire had demonstrated. The coverage also was very disorganized. Every parish bought its own coverage, often from a parishioner; there was no consistency in the amount or type of coverage. The types of coverage, the terms and limits, varied from parish to parish, and it was impossible for the archdiocese to get a clear picture of its insurance situation.

In addition, the archdiocese's unique legal makeup made it possible to consider combining property, liability and workers compensation coverages. At that time, the states prohibited separate entities from combining their liability risks under one program. However, the bishop of a diocese–or the cardinal of an arch-diocese–is the legal owner of all property and is legally responsible for all liability within the diocese, including the property and liability of the individual parishes. So the parishes were not separate entities, and they could combine their coverage.

Bob, John and Ed explained how the archdiocese could get its self-insurance started using the premium refunds it would get from canceling its parish policies. And, they told Bishop O'Donnell that the archdiocese would save more in pre-miums than the amount of its self-insured exposure. In other words, the archdio-cese couldn't end up paying more than it currently paid–and it might very well end up paying a lot less. O'Donnell and Klupar became important supporters of the Gallagher plan, which became known as the Bishop's Plan for Self-Insurance. At that time, self-insurance was a concept that either people understood or they didn't; O'Donnell and Klupar understood.

Klupar was a very astute layman who had been in charge of Catholic Cemeter-ies. He was famous for his financial conservatism–according to legend, he devel-oped a plan for digging large numbers of graves ahead of time and lowering the burial vaults into them, so that when there was a funeral, all that had to be done was move a little dirt.

Klupar understood the financial implications of self-insurance. But he under-stood the human savings as well. He was a very strong proponent of the concept of loss control; he believed that was one of the major benefits of self-insurance.

He had been deeply and personally distressed by the tragedy at Our Lady of the Angels–and especially by the feeling that it could have been, at least in part, prevented by better fire safety techniques. After all the claims from the fire were settled, he gave Bob Gallagher the photographs from the settlements, showing the injuries received by the victims.

"I showed those pictures to the safety engineers at Gallagher Bassett and I told them, 'This can never happen again,'" Bob recalled. "I still have those photos, in case we ever need to be reminded of the importance of what we do." In fact, AJGCo. now handles coverage for school districts representing about 15 million children nationwide, and there never has been a fatal fire at any of those schools.

At the urging of Klupar and O'Donnell, Cardinal Meyer told AJGCo. to go ahead and draw up the program. In May 1964, all the parishes were asked to send their policies to the chancery office. There were about 1,500 policies in all, from more than 450 parishes. Under the direction of John Gallagher, Gallagher Bas-sett hired extra help to audit the policies and to prepare cancellation forms. Each policy was kept and filed, in case problems arose later.

The Gallaghers also designed the type of coverage to be provided–in essence, creating an insurance policy. In the process, they made some very important decisions. For example, they designed coverage that included replacement costs. Up until that time, few insurers were willing to cover property replacement costs, because they felt replacement coverage presented too great a temptation for arson and fraud. However, self-insured clients had no such temptation, because they, rather than the insurance company, had to pay the retained losses.

The next step was to find excess coverage. No company in the United States would consider the coverage, so, on the Sunday before Thanksgiving in 1964, John Gallagher flew to London. He met with underwriters at Lloyd's of London on Monday and Tuesday, explaining the idea.

The excess coverage the Gallaghers were proposing was unique, because it combined property, casualty and workers compensation exposures and because it included replacement costs. However, the Lloyd's underwriters realized that the archdiocese was an unusual insured. Like any self-insured client, the archdiocese had no incentive to commit arson or fraud. In fact, it even had an extra incentive to keep losses low: As a religious entity, the archdiocese was tax-exempt, and therefore it got to keep 100 percent of anything it saved instead of having to pay half to the government in taxes.

On Tuesday, Julian Huxtable of the Sturge Syndicate agreed to become the lead signature on the insurance slip, ensuring that the rest of the slip would be filled. John put the slip in a safe and flew home for Thanksgiving.

Bob, Art, John, Sterling and Dan Wachs took the completed proposal to the cardinal, and he decided to implement the program, effective on February 1, 1965. The Bishop's Plan included a self-insured first working layer of $100,000, covering all property, casualty and workers compensation risks. The proposal was highly secret, kept under lock and key at the chancery office.

On February 1, when the archdiocese notified the individual parishes about the plan, all hell broke loose. The brokers at the parishes, who found their policies canceled, were furious. Many of them were loyal parishioners who had handled the insurance business of their parish for years–often at a discount–and they felt betrayed. The AJGCo. office at the time was in the Insurance Exchange building, and, Bob recalled, "There was a lot of conversation about us in the elevator." But the Gallaghers remained firm and the archdiocese remained committed, and eventually the objections died down.

The program ran smoothly, and the Gallaghers and Sterling realized that it could be adapted easily to other dioceses and archdioceses. They took the Bishop's Plan for Self-Insurance on the road.

The Bishop's Plan made AJGCo.–and Gallagher Bassett–a national name. Although Beatrice had locations around the country, the company was headquartered in Chicago and, up until this point, the Gallaghers had been essentially Chicago brokers. The Bishop's Plan changed that.

The first diocese to sign on after Chicago was the Diocese of Joliet. Joliet presented some new challenges, because it was a much smaller diocese than Chicago, with a much smaller spread of risk. The key to successful self-insurance is to have a good spread of risk, so the plan was adapted to the smaller diocese.

Once Joliet signed on, other dioceses followed: Gary, Indiana; San Antonio, Texas; Miami; Sacramento, California. The expansion of the Bishop's Plan was invaluable in proving that Arthur J. Gallagher & Co. could apply its new principles of risk management to many different situations in many different locations.

In San Antonio, for example, the diocese was heavily influenced by the farm workers unionization movement. Bob and Sterling made the presentation in San Antonio, and they had to meet with all the agents from all the parishes, because the diocese was committed to the concept of full representation.

John found the opposite to be true in New York, where Cardinal Francis Spellman ruled with an iron hand. When the bishops and other church officials gathered in Cardinal Spellman's conference room, there was a red light and a green light in front of each chair. When one of the church officials spoke, the green light came on; however, if the cardinal decided he had heard enough, he switched on the red light.

The Gallaghers certainly benefited from the fact that they were Catholic; they understood the Catholic mindset, and they were comfortable in the company of priests. Sterling, who was not Catholic, recalled that he often stepped back in discussions to let Bob or John take over.

The Gallaghers also shared a deep commitment to their church, and they were motivated in no small part by the belief that their plan was in the church's best interests. They remain committed; many of their individual philanthropic efforts still are directed toward Catholic causes.

But being good Irish Catholics was not enough to sell the Bishop's Plan. Neither was the fact that the plan provided the best coverage and the best control at by far the best price. When the Gallaghers took the Bishop's Plan on the road, they drew on the same talent for sales and professionalism that their father had tapped decades earlier.

In the late 1960s, for example, Bob, John, Sterling and Lou Metzger attended the Risk and Insurance Management Society Conference in San Francisco. After a few days of hobnobbing in the halls, they decided that there was not enough opportunity at RIMS for the four of them. Bob suggested that they make appointments with chancery offices up and down the California coast and get out and pitch the Bishop's Plan.

John and Sterling headed south, and Bob and Lou went north. Bob called the Diocese of Sacramento and told Monsignor Higgins that he would like to present a proposal for insurance that could save the diocese a substantial amount of money. The monsignor was reluctant, but Bob was persistent, promising that he would take no more than five minutes of Higgins' time. Finally, Higgins agreed to see Bob the following day at 1:30 in the afternoon.

Bob and Lou arrived at the office early, at about 1, and announced themselves to the secretary. It was a very small office, with only the secretary guarding the door to the office of Monsignor Higgins. No one came or went, and no phone calls came in, but the secretary did not send them in. The big clock on the wall ticked slowly, until finally it got around to 1:30, and the secretary told them that the monsignor would see them now.

The enforced wait annoyed Bob; after all, he had a plan that could save the diocese a fortune, and he was practically begging to be able to share it with Higgins. So when Bob and Lou were ushered into the office, Bob laid down a piece of paper showing how much the plan already was saving for dioceses that were using it.

"I know how busy you are, monsignor, but I just wanted to show you this," Bob said. "This is how much we have already saved the Catholic Church."

He left the paper on the desk for a minute or two while the monsignor looked it over, and then he picked it up.

"I know I told you that I would only take five minutes of your time, and you obviously are very busy today," Bob said, putting the paper away. "I'll come back when you have more time."

Monsignor Higgins, who was Irish-born, looked up at Bob and said in a heavy brogue, "Sit down, young man."

The Diocese of Sacramento bought the Bishop's Plan, and became an important ally for the plan with other dioceses. AJGCo. eventually sold the Bishop's Plan to about 100 dioceses and archdioceses around the country. Most of these, including the Archdiocese of Chicago, still use the plan decades later.

Every time a new diocese signed on, Gallagher Bassett created an office in that city to provide the personal service and attention that was becoming a hallmark of GB. Again, Sterling's ability to open an office on the run became very important. He had an exceptional ability to find the right people to staff the office and to work with the church. One of Sterling's first employees was Jim Enright, a respected property loss adjuster for General Adjustment. Enright in turn recruited many talented people for GB, including Jack Campbell, who led Gallagher Bassett after Sterling retired.

The GB offices in the dioceses also served Beatrice operations, if there were any in that location, and became the backbone of the Gallagher Bassett network. Today, there are more than 100 Gallagher Bassett offices throughout the United States.

By adapting the self-insurance plan created for Beatrice to fit the needs of religious entities, Gallagher Bassett pushed the alternative market a little further along. It would continue to push and to mold that market, as it applied self-insurance to public entities and to corporations.

Chapter 6
Driving The Wagon

"The art of becoming a member (of a corporation) is something more than a contract; it is entering into a complex and abiding relation."

Oliver Wendell Holmes Jr.

The growth of AJGCo. depended to a large extent on the growth of the sales force at the company. From the very beginning, AJGCo. planned for and took that growth seriously. The Gallaghers often say that some of their best ideas were forced upon them by circumstances, and AJGCo.'s aggressive and unique approach to training was at least partly a response to circumstances. But, as happened so many times, it was precisely the right response. Traditionally, insurance brokerages had two kinds of employees, other than clerical help. Salesmen did the actual selling, and technical employees placed the coverage and handled drawing up the policies and other paperwork and administrative tasks. This two-tiered system developed at least partly because the small brokerage system was extremely vulnerable to piracy. Before the emergence of the big, national brokerage firms, which now include AJGCo. among them, insurance was sold primarily by very small operations. A brokerage's top salesman could–and often did–decide to strike out on his own, taking with him many of his existing customers. By limiting the number of salesmen, a business owner limited his exposure; it was a kind of primitive risk management.

In the beginning, Arthur J. Gallagher & Co. operated in the traditional fashion: Art contacted the customers and sold the insurance, and Dan Wachs and Ed Keating did the technical work. But it soon became apparent to everyone that there were flaws in that setup. First of all, it restricted the opportunities for the technical people. Dan and Ed wanted to sell, they were talented insurance professionals, so why shouldn't they get a chance at sales–and at commissions?

In addition, technical people did not bring any money into the business, at least directly. They did free up the sales force to go out and sell, but they didn't generate any income for the company, which still had to pay them a salary. If they became producers, working on commission, their financial worth to the company would be increased greatly.

And Art was more than capable of handling his own placements and servicing; he had done it for years, before Dan and Ed came along. Many brokers needed the technical support because their expertise was in selling, not in working with the insurers. But Art had developed the skills and the contacts with insurers as well as with clients, and he was very comfortable in both worlds.

Soon, Dan and Ed were selling along with Art. And all of them were handling the technical side as well. When Jim, Bob and John Gallagher came into the company, they also handled both sales and the technical details, placing the coverage and servicing the policies. As a result, the Gallagher brothers learned all aspects of their business, and they learned quickly.

This worked well for a while, but eventually the Gallaghers realized that the company's growth was limited because they simply could not handle all the potential business. Art still spent much of the time in Florida, where he had gone to recover from rheumatic fever. Jim, Bob, John, Dan and Ed were selling practically around the clock, and they still could not keep up with demand. They had some office support: Florence Craig joined in 1951 as an assistant to Mabel Pottinger, and Lou Baldineri joined in 1961 in the accounting department. (Florence Craig is still with AJGCo., and Lou Baldineri retired after 30 years with the company; both watched their careers grow along with AJGCo., and contributed significantly to that growth.)

In the late 1950s, the Gallagher brothers began a series of sometimes-heated discussions about how to add to their staff. Jim spoke strongly in favor of expanding the sales force. He pointed out that in all the years of AJGCo.–including the war years, when virtually all the principals had been away–the company never had lost a client to piracy. He argued that adding salesmen would offer the best opportunity for the business to expand, and would relieve some of the pressure he and his brothers were under. "We've been pulling the wagon," he told them. "Why don't we learn to drive it?"

They agreed to add a producer, and Jim was put in charge of finding the right person for the job. This assignment was tailor-made for Jim, with his strong interest in management principles and organizational dynamics and structure.

The first step was determining what kind of salesman would be best for the company. The Gallaghers decided that the way they had developed as producers–learning both the technical and the sales sides of the business–was an important factor in their success as a company. The fact that they had achieved this dual expertise was an accident of circumstance, but they seized the opportunity to make circumstance work for them. "We clearly identified what we wanted our salesmen to do," Jim laughed. "We wanted them to become exactly what we were."

The Manpower Program that the Gallaghers developed under Jim's direction was designed to recruit and train salesmen "to become exactly what we were." In many ways, it was a revolutionary program. First, the fact that there was a formal program at all was revolutionary. In the late 1950s, companies–especially small ones–were run mostly by the seat of the pants. Management decisions were made only when some crisis arose, and were based almost entirely on the owner's "gut feeling." The Manpower Program, which was so official that it even had a name, was predicated on the idea that something as important as personnel selection and training should be planned and executed with care.

Also, the program was unusual because it involved a commitment of money. The Gallaghers agreed to take part of each year's profit and earmark it for increasing the sales force the following year.

This was especially significant because AJGCo., like most small companies, "bonused out" its profits. At the end of the year, the company would figure how much it had in profit and then would, in essence, divvy up that profit among the principals. In this way, the company would have no profit on which to pay taxes. So using some of the profit for personnel development was literally taking that money out of the pockets of Jim, Bob, John, Dan and Ed. This became, in a very real sense, a matter of putting your money where your mouth is.

Also unlike many other insurance brokerages at that time, the Gallaghers decided to present their program to area colleges and universities. The Gallaghers were college-educated, and they believed in the value of higher education. They also felt that if a person had finished college, it was evidence of above-average intelligence and commitment to seeing things through.

Once they had recruited the right trainees, they decided, they would put them directly into the fire. The agency had a small book of personal lines business, most of it handled by Mabel Pottinger. This was very low-risk business, mainly because it represented such a tiny fraction of the agency's total revenue. The Gallaghers decided that each trainee would be given a number of existing personal lines accounts to handle. The trainee would be responsible for servicing those accounts and for getting the renewals.

After he was comfortable with that, he was expected to try to sell more personal lines business, by expanding the contacts he had made through his existing business and developing new contacts. Eventually, he would move into commercial lines—which remained by far the agency's largest business—and turn his book of personal lines accounts over to the next trainee.

The payment plan for the trainees was designed to ease them into a compensation formula the Gallaghers developed based on production. The Gallaghers believed that, although the production-based formula offered the best opportunity to make a lot of money in insurance, it could be tough for young producers to have to rely on it immediately. So Gallagher recruits were paid a base salary and given some business to work with.

As they began to bring in more business, their salary was supplemented by a bonus determined by the Gallaghers' formula. Eventually, as their sales abilities grew, the recruits were paid entirely according to the production-based formula. In this way, young trainees would not starve while they were learning the ropes, but they would find out quite soon that the real money came with increasing the book of business.

Jim took the Manpower Program to the heads of the placement offices at the major Chicago universities, telling them that he had a program that would teach young people how to make a good living in the insurance business. The head of placement at DePaul University was less than enthusiastic about Jim's offer. He told Jim that he could not in good conscience recommend to any of his promising graduates that they try insurance brokerage, because that business had a reputation for chewing up bright young men and spitting them out.

Jim was determined to prove him wrong. He believed that the Manpower Program offered the right person an excellent chance at success. He and his brothers had designed the program specifically to give trainees a solid foundation in all aspects of the industry, and to provide them with both financial security while they learned the business and an opportunity to make a substantial income if they learned well and worked hard.

Ironically, the first recruit under the Manpower Program was from DePaul. Tom Cloutier came to work for AJGCo. on November 1, 1961, and from the very beginning, he took the office by storm. He was very successful with his personal lines business, and began to move into commercial lines. But sadly, on January 15, 1964, Tom Cloutier died of cancer.

The Manpower Program evolved into the company's highly successful Summer Internship Program. The startup of the Summer Internship Program owed much to the personal involvement of John Gallagher, who used his strong instinct for finding talented people and then made them feel at home and appreciated at the company. Cubs games, barbecues and get-togethers at John's home became a traditional part of the program that continues to this day. And John Gallagher still tries to interview and meet with all interns during the course of the program. Like the Manpower Program, the Summer Internship Program focuses on teaching young people all aspects of the business, on giving them responsibility teamed with guidance, and on helping them to determine if this business and this company are for them.

George McWeeney took over the Summer Internship Program in 1980, when he joined AJGCo. as Director of Training. McWeeney, who came to AJGCo. after nine years with Liberty Mutual Insurance Company and 14 years with Allstate, ran the internship program with exceptional success. In 1983 he was named a corporate officer as Vice President of Operational Support. He became invaluable in a host of ways, ranging from writing the annual report to orchestrating the annual shareholders and marketing meetings, to designing seminars, to writing sales brochures. Even after his retirement in 1993, he continued to work with AJGCo. in an advisory capacity.

The Summer Internship Program that John Gallagher and McWeeney put together offers summer employment to young people after their sophomore year of college, and again after their junior year. If both the company and the intern are happy with the arrangement, the intern is offered a job at AJGCo. after graduation.

Jim Gault, who now heads the National Risk Management Sales division of AJGCo., started as an intern in the summer of 1972, after his sophomore year of college. "It was my first coat-and-tie job," he remembered. His intern class included, among others, Patrick Gallagher, now president and CEO of the company, and Peter Durkalski, now president of Gallagher Bassett.

Gault spent part of his time with producers, and part of his time working for Gallagher Bassett doing inspections for parishes covered by the Bishop's Plan. He learned how to spot a loose stair rail, but he also learned the value of customer service. He came to realize that his presence, representing Gallagher Bassett to the parish priest, was probably at least as important as his advice.

And in fact, intangibles such as customer service and corporate culture were–and are–vital parts of the Summer Internship Program. AJGCo. wants to teach its interns not only about the details of insurance brokerage, but also about the company, its people and its values.

"The training program was a little like a fraternity rush, exposing you to the business and to the guys–because in those days they were almost all guys, although now about 40 percent of the interns are women," Gault recalled. "The program always seemed to be asking, 'What do you think about these guys? Are these the kinds of guys you'd like to work with?'" Gault decided the answer was yes, and when John Gallagher wrote and offered him a job in the fall of his senior year, he gladly accepted.

The job was to begin in September of 1974. John told Gault, as he told all his intern hires, that he should not start work until the end of the summer after graduation, because it would be a long time before he would get another chance to spend three months doing whatever he wanted. Gault actually started on July 15, 1974. He had spent two months traveling around the country until his money ran out, so he called John and asked if he could start early. He never has looked back.

The program has continued to evolve in the years since Gault was an intern, but it has remained focused on the same goal: giving promising young people a chance to learn about an industry and a company. Like the early trainees in the

Manpower Program, today's interns learn by doing. And, true to the commitment they made in the late 1950s, the Gallaghers continue to believe that finding and training a sales force is worth spending time and money on.

The Summer Internship Program can be measured by the success of the people who have gone through it. About 70 percent of the people who passed through the internship program are still with the company, and many of them are in top positions: About 19 people who currently hold senior management positions at Gallagher are alumni of the internship program.

Some of those interns, like Patrick Gallagher, Bob Gallagher Jr., Tom Gallagher, Jennifer Gallagher, and Gary, Craig and Warren Van der Voort Jr., may well have come to AJGCo. anyway because it was the company of their fathers. Others, like Gault, Durkalski and Clark Johnson, area president, Los Angeles, found a career during those summers.

For all of them, though, the internship program did what it was designed to do: It gave them a taste of AJGCo., and it helped them decide if they wanted to take a bigger bite.

Gallagher Gallery I

After enlisting in 1917 in the Army's Illinois 33rd Division, 108th Engineers, Arthur J. Gallagher served with distinction in France under General "Black Jack" Pershing.

Top: Art Gallagher (left center) was part of a multinational force in France during World War I. Bottom left: Art enjoyed a rare quiet moment in camp. Bottom right: Art (top left) served with his childhood friend Eddie Daly (bottom left), who later became superintendent of detectives in Chicago.

In his wartime diary, Art Gallagher recorded the fear and excitement of a young man under fire and far from home.

The first office of Arthur J. Gallagher & Co. was located in the Insurance
Exchange building in Chicago's Loop.

MRS ARTHUR JAMES GALLAGHER.
PHOTO · WALINGER.

Mrs. Patrick James Madden of 912 Buena avenue announces the marriage of her daughter, Katherine, to Arthur James Gallagher. The ceremony took place yesterday. Mr. and Mrs. Gallagher will be at home after June 1 at 7044 Greenview avenue.

Left: After Art Gallagher returned from France as an officer and a gentleman, he married Katherine Madden on April 22, 1920. Top right: Ten years later, in 1930, the couple struck an affectionate pose. Bottom right: But they were no longer alone. They had been joined by their children (from left) John, Kate, Bob and Jim.

The Gallagher family showed off its Sunday best. Katherine and Art, in the back row, are joined by (front from left) Bob, Kate, John, Jim (in back) and family friend Dick Kullman, a future Gallagher Bassett employee.

Art and Katherine Gallagher stroll around the Dairyman's Country Club in Boulder Junction, Wisconsin, in 1939.

All three of the Gallagher sons served in the U.S. Navy during World War II. Top left: John joined after graduation from high school in 1945. Bottom left: Bob qualified as a carrier dive bomber pilot. Right: Jim served in the South Pacific in Naval Air Transport.

Top: The lineup of producers at AJGCo. after the war was (from left) John Gallagher, Ed Keating, Jim Gallagher, Dan Wachs and Bob Gallagher. Bottom: Relaxing after a round of golf in 1949 were (from left) John, Jim, Art and Bob Gallagher.

Top: In the early 1950s, the staff labored in an office "pit" in the Insurance Exchange building. Bottom left: Mabel Pottinger, hired in 1928, was a guiding force in Arthur J. Gallagher & Co. for more than four decades; this photo is from 1952. Bottom right: By 1958, Art Gallagher (right) was relying heavily on his sons (from left) Bob, Jim and John.

Top left: By the early 1970s, the growing agency had moved into larger quarters at 1 East Wacker Drive. From these offices, AJGCo. directed the Bishop's Plan for Self-Insurance. Top right: Cardinal Albert G. Meyer (left) and Bishop Cletus O'Donnell were instrumental in the adoption of the Bishop's Plan by the Archdiocese of Chicago. Spearheading the plan at Gallagher were Sterling Bassett (bottom left) and John Gallagher (bottom right).

How one agency is solving its recruiting needs through a unique training program for college students

An article from the mid-1970s touted the innovative Summer Internship Program. Featured in this photo were (from left) Patrick Gallagher, Walter Larkin, Craig Van der Voort, Gary Van der Voort, Bob Gallagher Jr., Peter Durkalski and Michael Platt. Only Platt no longer is with the company.

Top AJGCo. management, including (from left) Sterling Bassett, Warren G. Van der Voort Sr., Dan Wachs, Jim Gallagher, John Gallagher and Bob Gallagher, struck a holiday pose in the company's new offices in the Gould Center. Inset: AJGCo. moved into the Gould Center, in Rolling Meadows, in 1976.

Top: Gallagher, Hinton & Vereker managers David Vereker (back) and Michael Vaughan-Fowler took an unusual form of transportation to Lloyd's of London in 1976. Bottom left: Dan Wachs was a young man when his neighbor, Art Gallagher, asked him to join Art's young company, and Wachs became a vital part of AJGCo.'s growth for decades. Bottom right: Bert Mochel's agency in Downers Grove, Illinois, was one of the first firms to join AJGCo. through acquisition.

Top: The culture of Arthur J. Gallagher & Co. always has relied heavily on a strong sense of family. The Gallagher family, gathered in the early 1980s, included (back row, from left) MaryClaire (Mrs. John) Gallagher, Katherine Gallagher Carani, Isabel (Mrs. Bob) Gallagher, Joseph Carani, Jim Gallagher, Bob Gallagher and John Gallagher, and (front row, from left) Marie (Mrs. Jim) Gallagher, and Katherine and Art Gallagher. Bottom: In 1983, Mary Claire, John, Isabel and Bob Gallagher joined Katherine and Art to celebrate the company's first $50 million sales year.

Top: The 1987 gathering of the branch managers revealed how much Arthur J. Gallagher & Co. had grown. Bottom: But in many important ways, it remained the same company that longtime employee Lou Baldineri (right), shown receiving a Certificate of Excellence from John Gallagher, had joined in 1961.

On December 1, 1987, Bob Gallagher accepted congratulations as the stock of Arthur J. Gallagher & Co. was first traded on the New York Stock Exchange. He is joined by Jay Mahoney (right) of A.C. Partners, AJGCo.'s market maker, and John K. Lyden (left) of the New York Stock Exchange board.

Top: The branch managers gathered in 1988. Bottom left: In 1985, top AJGCo. managers including (from left) Warren Van der Voort Sr., Dan Wachs and Sterling Bassett attended a stockholders meeting. Bottom right: In 1986, John Gallagher (left) was executive vice president, and Bob Gallagher was president and CEO.

By the mid-1980s, AJGCo. was powered by young managers with a long history. Top: Walt McClure (left), chairman of Brokerage Services, joined AJGCo. in 1976. John Stancik, head of the London operations, came aboard in 1970. Bottom left: Jack Campbell joined Gallagher Bassett in 1969, moving up to chairman in 1988. Bottom right: Frank Heffernan (left) merged his San Francisco agency into AJGCo. in 1986. Bill Jensen (center) joined AJGCo. in 1971 and rose to senior vice president. Gary Van der Voort (right), a former summer intern, became president of Brokerage Services.

The original board of directors after Arthur J. Gallagher & Co. became a public company was made up of: (top from left) Robert E. Gallagher, John P. Gallagher, J. Patrick Gallagher Jr. and Robert H.B. Baldwin; (middle from left) John G. Campbell, Michael J. Cloherty, Jack M. Greenberg; (bottom from left) Walter F. McClure and James R. Wimmer.

In 1989, other corporate officers for AJGCo. were: (top from left) James W. Durkin Jr., Joseph W. Fahey, Frank M. Heffernan Jr., David B. Hoch; (middle from left) Bill G. Jensen, David R. Long, George A. McWeeney and John D. Stancik; (bottom from left) Mark P. Strauch, Gary M. Van der Voort and Warren G. Van der Voort Jr.

Top: There were many familiar faces at the 1989 branch managers meeting. Bottom: Also in 1989, ground was broken for the new Gallagher Centre in Itasca. Wielding shovels were (from left) John, Patrick and Bob Gallagher, and Mike Cloherty.

The board of directors in 1991 consisted of (back row from left) Michael
J. Cloherty, Philip A. Marineau and Robert H.B. Baldwin; (middle from
left) John G. Campbell, J. Patrick Gallagher Jr. and Jack M. Greenberg;
and (front from left) John P. Gallagher, Robert E. Gallagher, James R.
Wimmer and Walter F. McClure.

The decade of the '90s dawned bright for Arthur J. Gallagher & Co. Top: Patrick Gallagher (left) was president and chief operating officer, and Bob Gallagher was chairman and CEO. Bottom right: The company had moved into its new home, the Gallagher Centre, in Itasca. Bottom left: Gallagher Bassett was entering a new era of independence, under the direction of its Executive Committee (from left) Richard J. McKenna, Richard R. Rothman, Peter J. Durkalski, Jack H. Lazzaro, Fred Potenza and Donald C. Klein.

Left: Cindy Franklin, from the Chicago Metro office in Downers Grove, was the top producer in 1991 and 1992. Right: George McWeeney joined the company in 1980 and handled a wide variety of tasks, from the Summer Internship Program to operational support to marketing and the annual report.

Bob Gallagher always has relied strongly on loyal employees such as Rosemarie Martin (right), his secretary for many years, and Florence Craig (inset), who joined the company in 1951 as an assistant to Mabel Pottinger.

Left: The Summer Internship Program trained many young people who went on to hold management positions at Arthur J. Gallagher & Co., including Jim Gault (left) and Clark Johnson, who are both vice presidents. Right: Jim Keough, area president for the Chicago Metro region, is a two-time winner of the coveted Brokerage Services Branch Manager of the Year Award.

AJGCo. continues to fill the ranks of its corporate officers from among its top young managers. Top: From left, David R. Long, vice president; Christine D. Greb, assistant secretary; and Mark P. Strauch, treasurer. Bottom left: Nicholas M. Elsberg, vice president. Bottom right: David E. McGurn Jr., vice president.

Top: Arthur J. Gallagher & Co.'s financial team includes (from left) Earl Warner, David Hoch and Robert Mason. Bottom: James W. Durkin Jr. (left), vice president—Gallagher Benefit Services, and Bette J. Brinkerhoff, vice president—Human Resources, are part of the team of corporate officers.

Patrick Gallagher (center), named president in 1990 and chief executive officer in 1995, is the third generation to lead the company his grandfather founded. Patrick's father, John (left), is the vice chairman of AJGCo. Patrick's uncle, Bob, is the chairman of the board.

Chapter 7
The Wild, Wild '70s

"A great wind is blowing, and that gives you either imagination or a headache."

Catherine the Great, empress of Russia

The growing sales force of Arthur J. Gallagher & Co. had a sure winner in the Bishop's Plan for Self-Insurance, and they made the most of it. The Bishop's Plan was a new, creative and innovative product that was fairly priced and met clients' needs; soon AJGCo. salespeople were traveling all over the country, selling the plan by airplane, while GB opened offices on the fly. • The concept of the Bishop's Plan also was well-suited for municipalities, park districts, school districts and similar entities. As tax-exempt entities like the dioceses, municipalities had a financial incentive to control losses. Being servants of the people–or at least of the political process–they had public relations reasons to promote safety. They could not merely raise prices to cover their insurance expenses. And in the 1970s, they already were beginning to feel the early tremors of the insurance market contraction that would hit with a vengeance in the early 1980s. • The company was opening offices at a furious pace to service the new business, especially the Bishop's Plan. There was little time to plan–everyone was too busy selling–so a lot of decisions were made on instinct. However, that instinct was usually right.

Jack Campbell, who now is chairman of Gallagher Bassett, was one of the many people who joined the company during this go-go period. He was hired in February 1969, after a lunch meeting with Sterling Bassett. "We just hit it off right away," Campbell said. "We were going to sweep the world."

At first, though, there wasn't much to sweep. Through the summer, things were very quiet, and Campbell began to wonder when the action would start. Then, right before Thanksgiving in 1969, the Diocese of Rockford, Illinois, called and set up an appointment for the Friday after Thanksgiving to give an order for the Bishop's Plan. John Gallagher called Campbell and said that he would pick Campbell up at home on Friday to drive to Rockford.

Campbell and his wife, Geri, had Thanksgiving dinner, and then Geri Campbell spent the rest of the night cleaning the house, making it ready for John's arrival the next morning. After all, she thought, the boss was coming over, and she wanted him to know she kept a nice house. When John came, though, he went to the back door and into the kitchen for a cup of coffee. "It was probably the warmest thing he could have done, but he never did see the house," Jack Campbell laughed.

In May, all the dioceses in the state of Michigan decided to join the plan, too, and Campbell went to Lansing to start a Gallagher Bassett office to service those dioceses. In the Gallagher tradition of getting involved in all aspects of the business, everyone in the new Lansing office pitched in and did everything, including licking stamps and hand-canceling policies.

In 1974, the Archdiocese of New York signed on to the Bishop's Plan, followed by the dioceses of Rockville Centre and Brooklyn, and Campbell was tapped to open an office in the New York metro area.

The experience of serving New York was typical of the way Gallagher Bassett met and overcame obstacles as the company wrote the book on self-insurance. From a small office in the Westchester County town of Mamaroneck, GB struggled with the difficult regulatory environment in New York.

First, the state required that Gallagher Bassett, which then was called Gallagher Bassett Insurance Services, remove the word "insurance" from its name. Then, regulators insisted that someone at GB be licensed by the state to handle workers compensation claims; Campbell went to classes, took his test and got his workers compensation license.

The real challenge came when the regulators determined that they would not license the workers compensation part of the self-insurance plan for the Archdiocese of New York until they saw the financial records of the archdiocese. The archdiocese was adamant that as a religious entity, it did not have to show its financials to the state, and for a while, it looked as if the whole deal would fall through.

Finally, a devoted Catholic woman who worked in the state workers compensation office, and who also had the ear of the cardinal, came to believe that the Bishop's Plan would be in the best interest of the archdiocese. She became an emissary to the cardinal, and eventually she persuaded both the cardinal and the state to allow her–and only her–to view the records. Her report satisfied the regulators, and no one else outside the archdiocese ever saw the records again.

The growth of self-insurance took the company across the country, and it also took AJGCo. across the Atlantic, to London, the home of Lloyd's. The Lloyd's market was critical to the success of self-insurance, because it handled the excess coverage; excess coverage, in effect, capped a client's potential losses and made clients more comfortable with the financial risk they were undertaking through self-insurance.

In the beginning, AJGCo. placed its business at Lloyd's with Lloyd's broker Stewart-Smith. But Stewart-Smith required AJGCo. to go through an affiliated office in Chicago. The Gallaghers did not mind paying Stewart-Smith a commission for its services, but they objected strongly to giving the Chicago office a cut in return for, in essence, being an order-taker.

Bob and John Gallagher went to London to seek an agreement to place the business directly with the Stewart-Smith home office, bypassing the Chicago operation. They thought they had arranged such a deal, but by the time they got back to Chicago from London, the deal was off, torpedoed by the objections of the Chicago office.

In response to the rebuff from Stewart-Smith, the Gallaghers turned right around and went back to London, where they formed Gallagher, Hinton & Vereker Ltd. At first, it was a subsidiary company of Lloyd's broker Hinton, Hill & Colls, with David Vereker as managing director. AJGCo. owned 56.5 percent of Gallagher, Hinton & Vereker when it was created on October 1, 1974, although AJGCo. later bought the rest of the company.

"Some of the best decisions we ever made, other people made for us, and this was one of them," John Gallagher said.

In 1981, Gallagher, Hinton & Vereker became the first subsidiary of a U.S. broker to be accepted as a Lloyd's broker in its own right.

Under the direction of John Gallagher, AJGCo. continued to expand its presence at Lloyd's with the 1986 purchase of John Plumer & Partners and the formation of Gallagher Plumer Ltd., which is now called Arthur J. Gallagher & Co. UK Ltd. The London operation is headed by John Stancik, the first U.S. citizen to manage the London office. Stancik was recruited by John Gallagher to join AJGCo. in 1970 as an account executive. He became a unit manager, headed the New York office and led the National Risk Management Sales division before crossing the Atlantic.

The presence in London is extremely important for AJGCo. because London is an integral part of the alternative market–a market that AJGCo. has claimed as its major niche. In addition, Arthur J. Gallagher & Co. UK Ltd. places business for other clients. In fact, more than half of its revenue comes from outside Arthur J. Gallagher & Co., making it an important contributor to the bottom line in its own right.

AJGCo. expanded not only to London, but also offshore in the 1970s. In 1975, the company established Arthur J. Gallagher & Co. (Bermuda) Ltd., which provided direct access to the important offshore insurance and reinsurance markets. Today the Bermuda operation is a central piece of a new Gallagher initiative into captive management.

In 1976, the company moved from its Chicago offices at 1 East Wacker Drive to the Gould Center in the suburb of Rolling Meadows. Bill Stenstrom, the personnel director at the time, spearheaded the move, getting employees involved and excited about moving to the suburbs.

Many other companies have since followed AJGCo. to the area west of Chicago, but at the time, the company almost literally was blazing a trail. And that trail didn't sit well with at least one Chicagoan.

When then-Mayor Richard J. Daley, with whom the Gallaghers had a very good relationship, heard the news, he called Bob Gallagher into his office and said, "I heard you're moving out. You can't do that."

Bob said, "I am, your honor. I signed a lease." To which Daley replied, "Then unsign the damn lease."

Bob assured him that the Gallaghers would always be Chicagoans and they would always support the city. Daley snorted, "Then support us in the city."

Despite Hizzoner's objections, AJGCo. did move to Rolling Meadows, and later to Itasca. But, true to Bob's word, the Gallaghers always have thought of themselves as Chicagoans. Chicago is their city, and they cut their teeth on her vitality and her infamous politics.

For example, after the riots following the death of Dr. Martin Luther King Jr., the Chicago Board of Education asked AJGCo. to put together coverage for the Chicago public schools. AJGCo. designed the coverage and won the business, but a few years later, the company found itself under attack by the Citizens Action Party. This group claimed the Board of Education was paying too much for its coverage, especially considering that there never had been a loss.

Reporters showed up at the AJGCo. offices, which still were at 1 East Wacker, and Bob invited them in. He positioned himself at his father's desk ("It was a much nicer desk than mine," he recalled.), and told the TV cameras to roll.

Bob smiled in a conciliatory way and said that he could understand the concern of the Citizens Action Party. After all, he said, "I pay a lot of life insurance premiums–and I thank God I haven't had a loss on my policy." The cameras stopped, the sound bite was captured, and the critics were answered.

Large municipal entities like the Chicago school system could go to self-insurance. But by the end of the decade, smaller cities and public entities were clamoring to be able to enjoy the benefits of the new markets. Once again, AJGCo. began to fashion a solution to this problem.

In the late 1970s, under the leadership of Bert Mochel and Warren Van der Voort Jr., AJGCo. pioneered the first self-insurance pool for public entities. Pooling allowed small, similar entities to join with other like entities to form a pool, creating a larger spread of risk. The Intergovernmental Risk Management Agency (IRMA) was followed by other pools, and a whole new world of possibilities–for broker and client alike–opened up.

Another avenue of growth that began to develop during this period was the employee benefits arena. In 1975, Gallagher's benefits division wrote the company's first self-funded employee benefits plan; this has become a major business line for AJGCo.

Also during the 1970s, the Gallagher brothers sold the first shares of stock to employees, and Jim Gallagher spearheaded several mergers, most notably the Mochel Agency in Downers Grove, which is now the Chicago Metro office.

All in all, the decade of the '70s was a period of incredible and unbridled growth for Arthur J. Gallagher & Co. It seemed as if everywhere the company turned, it uncovered new opportunities. And it transformed those opportunities into reality.

Arthur J. Gallagher & Co. recorded its first year of more than $1 million in revenues in 1968, more than 40 years after Art Gallagher took his leave of Moore Case Lyman & Hubbard. In 1978–only 10 years later–the company reported almost $25 million in revenues.

Throughout the 1970s, average annual revenue growth was 36 percent, average annual earnings growth was 56 percent, and average annual staff growth was 27 percent. The company added 10 new branch offices around the country, and established a presence in London and in Bermuda.

Those were wild and exciting times. "We were breaking new ground everywhere we went," Warren Van der Voort Jr. remembered. "We were running around everywhere, wherever we could sell something."

The whirlwind young sales force included Patrick Gallagher, who joined the company in 1974, after he graduated from Cornell. He remembered his first account: Aurora Equipment Co., which paid him $2,000 in commission. "I was hooked," he said.

Actually, Patrick had been hooked since he first came to the company, in the summer of 1966, when he was 14 and served as a second-generation "go-fer" for Mabel Pottinger. Since that time, he knew that he wanted to be part of the company his grandfather, his father and his uncles had built.

When he was in college, Patrick joined the internship program, spending a summer in the Chicago office and a summer in London. After graduation, Patrick got married, and his wife, Anne, was not sure she wanted him to accept the insecurity of sales, with its income based on production, rather than a regular paycheck somewhere else. Patrick persuaded her, though, that AJGCo. was where he wanted to go.

The '70s was a perfect decade for an enthusiastic young recruit like Patrick Gallagher, and in a few years he was salesman of the year. All the top executives and salespeople went on a company trip to Hawaii–one of several such trips the company made during those free-spending years. Patrick was sitting at a company luau in Hawaii with Anne, who was pregnant with their first child. They were enjoying the beautiful surroundings when a company-paid helicopter began to circle overhead, dropping orchid petals.

Patrick recalled that he looked at his wife and said, "How do you think we're doing now?"

Indeed, the whole company was doing very well, basking in its success as the curtain fell on the '70s–and prepared to rise on a new decade, with new challenges and new opportunities.

Chapter 8
Going Public

"The wise man understands equity; the small man understands only profits."

Confucius

In 1981, Mike Cloherty and Bob Gallagher sat down to dinner in New York City. By the end of the evening, they had cemented a relationship that would become vital in helping to move Arthur J. Gallagher & Co. into a new era. • Cloherty first talked to Bob in 1980, when he interviewed for a job as vice president of finance at AJGCo. He didn't get the job, but a year later, Bob called him again. The man who had been hired had not worked out, Bob said, and he wanted to know if he could fly out to New York and talk to Cloherty again. "I was very impressed that he would fly all the way out to New York to take me out to dinner," Cloherty recalled. • At the time, Cloherty was still in his mid-30s, and the Number 2 financial official at broker Frank B. Hall. He was looking for a change from Hall, and he had been impressed during his interview with Bob a year earlier and disappointed at not getting the job. Over dinner in 1981, Cloherty asked Bob why he had not been hired. "Was I too young?" Cloherty asked. "No," Bob replied, "I just blew it." • Bob didn't make the same mistake twice, and Cloherty joined AJGCo. Very shortly, he found that he had his work cut out for him.

When Cloherty had been with the company about a week, he was looking down from his office in the Gould Center onto the complex tennis courts, watching the AJGCo. brokers playing tennis in the sunshine. "I thought, What a wonderful place to work," Cloherty said. "A few days later, I discovered that I would have to borrow money to make the payroll."

It wasn't that the company was broke; it was simply that the cash was not available to cover the checks. During the wide-open '70s, the company had developed a reputation for working hard and playing hard. There was a fleet of BMWs and corporate sales incentive trips to exotic locales.

Cloherty came into this environment with a clear directive from Bob Gallagher: Bring professional financial discipline to this company, and get it ready to go public.

Bob also had determined that financial discipline had to go hand-in-hand with more professional management, including long-term strategic planning. He called in a well-known corporate consultant, Dr. Ram Charan, and working with Charan he established profit centers and imposed more financial and management accountability on the various operations.

Many managers in the company, long accustomed to running their own shows, were leery of or openly hostile toward the financial discipline and the management changes. But Bob believed that these changes were necessary in order to prepare the organization to meet the new challenges it would face; he held fast to his position, and he ultimately accomplished the redirection he sought.

"We had to change from a freewheeling company to a professionally managed company," Cloherty said. "It was a little like making a U-turn with the Queen Mary: It took time and a lot of ocean, but we did it."

The U-turn was necessary in order to point AJGCo. in a new direction, toward being a public company. Going public had long been a dream of the Gallaghers. James R. Wimmer, an attorney specializing in corporate law with the Chicago firm of Lord, Bissell & Brook, who later became a member of the AJGCo. board, recalled first talking to Bob about going public around 1970.

"At that time the company had total assets of about $10 million, and I remember telling him, 'I don't think you're a candidate yet,'" Wimmer said. "But he never gave up on the idea, and he kept working toward it."

In 1970, the company stock was privately held by the Gallaghers. During that decade, the brothers agreed to take some of their shares and distribute them to Dan Wachs, Ed Keating, Sterling Bassett, Warren Van der Voort Sr., and the employee profit-sharing plan. Later they distributed shares to other people who had become very important to the development of the company, and they began to issue financial reports to those shareholders, as if they were a public company.

Bob developed a formula for determining the value of the shares, based on a multiple of the prior two years' earnings. The company bought back the shares when a shareholder died or left, and it also agreed to buy back the stock of any shareholder who decided he no longer wanted the investment.

As the company and the number of shareholders grew, the company's potential financial obligation also increased. By 1984, there were about 100 shareholders; if the shareholders all had decided to turn in their stock, the company could have faced financial ruin. As a public company, this danger would be eliminated.

Going public would increase the net worth of the company, and it would provide increased name recognition for AJGCo. and its products and services. Being a public company also would ensure that AJGCo. would be talked about and studied by the financial community as well as the insurance industry, and the company welcomed that scrutiny and exposure.

Bob also wanted to go public for philosophical reasons. He wanted to create a mechanism that would allow AJGCo. employees to share in the success they were creating. That had been the motivation behind the original decision to issue stock to key employees, and Bob wanted to expand that opportunity throughout the company.

Jack Campbell remembered talking to Bob after the public offering had been completed in 1984. Bob had spent an enormous amount of time and energy on the public offering, and Campbell said to him, "Why did you put yourself through this? You and your family are financially set for life; why go to all this effort?" Bob replied, "This company is about more than the Gallaghers, and I want everyone who contributed to the company to benefit as well."

When Cloherty came on board in 1981, he focused all his efforts on establishing the financial discipline that would allow the company to realize Bob's dream. The first step was to get control of expenses.

"For a long time, I was a very unpopular person around here," Cloherty laughed. "I was the guy whose job it was to say no—no to the trips, no to the unrestrained expense accounts. But to a broker, there is really no such thing as no—there is only a new challenge."

Cloherty, with the full support of Bob, did say no, and he began to issue practice filings and financials. Under Cloherty's direction, the company set up the accounting structure required of a public company.

There were many companies ready and willing to take Arthur J. Gallagher & Co. public, and Bob eventually chose Morgan Stanley & Co. He was impressed with Morgan Stanley's professional expertise. And, in another of the odd twists of fate that characterize the Gallagher story, Bob was very comfortable with Morgan Stanley's chairman, Robert H. B. Baldwin.

Bob Gallagher and Bob Baldwin had played basketball against each other years before in the Ivy League, when Bob Gallagher was at Cornell and Bob Baldwin was at Princeton. Bob Gallagher had not kept in personal touch with Baldwin, but he had watched his old adversary's career. After graduating summa cum laude in 1942 from Princeton with a Phi Beta Kappa key and varsity letters in football, baseball and basketball, Baldwin had joined the U.S. Navy. In 1946, after World War II, he left active Navy service and joined Morgan Stanley, becoming a partner in 1958, president in 1973 and chairman in 1983. He also served as Undersecretary of the Navy from 1965 to 1967.

Baldwin was a man whose personal and professional accomplishments Bob Gallagher could relate to and admire, and a man whom Bob trusted to take his company public. In 1985, Baldwin became one of AJGCo.'s first outside directors.

In an unusual case of bad timing, AJGCo. was ready to go public in early 1984, just when the insurance industry experienced a crisis of cost and availability that landed it on the cover of Time magazine. Bob negotiated with T. Kimball Brooker, the head of the Chicago office of Morgan Stanley, an initial offering price of between $18 and $21 per share. However, there was little public interest or underwriting syndicate support in this price range. Bob and Morgan started cutting the price and, on June 4, 1984, the initial offering was completed on the NASDAQ at a price of $13.75.

Several years later, a friend of Bob's remarked that Morgan Stanley had done Gallagher a disservice in pricing the issue so low. Bob disagreed strongly, saying, "The 80 percent of my shares that I kept are eternally grateful to the 20 percent of my shares I sold, which started the process." By 1995, after a 2-for-1 stock split that occurred in 1986, the value of the stock had increased by 442 percent.

In 1995, 11 years after the initial public offering, T. Kimball Brooker became a member of the board of directors of Arthur J. Gallagher & Co., upon the retirement of Bob Baldwin. Previously, Philip A. Marineau, then president of Quaker Oats, had joined the AJGCo. board.

In 1987, AJGCo. joined the New York Stock Exchange, listing 10.9 million shares of common stock on The Big Board. Jim Gallagher recalled going to a dinner party to celebrate the listing of the company on the New York Stock Exchange. Among the guests at the party was an analyst whom Jim had called in 1972 to talk about Gallagher Bassett and the possibilities offered by self-insurance. At the time, the analyst had been very skeptical about the future of self-insurance.

At the dinner, the analyst sought Jim out to admit his mistake. "You told me then that your company was going to grow at 15 percent a year indefinitely, and it has done that or more for the last 15 years," the analyst said. "Now tell me—what's it going to do for the next 15 years?"

AJGCo. continued to grow, of course. And in the process it gained the respect of analysts and investors alike, in large part because, from the very beginning, the company was committed to keeping to its own agenda and to being honest with the financial community. At first, Bob Gallagher and Cloherty handled all the analyst contact. They were open about the company's triumphs, but they also were frank when problems came up. They refused to sacrifice the company's long-term goals to meet quarterly expectations.

They provided a reliable, honest appraisal, not only of their company, but also of their industry. Even today, analysts who follow the insurance industry often consult with AJGCo. about trends within the industry, because they have come to know that AJGCo. is important in setting those trends, and will provide valuable insight into where the industry is headed.

AJGCo. management always has believed that one of the best investments the company could make was in itself. Starting in 1985 and continuing through

1995, the company has invested $110 million by repurchasing more than 4 million of its shares.

As the Gallaghers hoped, going public has allowed the company's employees to benefit from the success they help to create. Almost one-fourth of the shares of AJGCo. are held by employees, officers and directors of the company; this does not include the holdings of the Gallagher family, who own 15 percent to 17 percent of the shares.

Bob estimates that scores of people have become millionaires as a result of their investment in AJGCo., and he is justly proud of that. But he is equally proud of the fact that many other employees have found financial security and a sense of ownership in the company through its employee stock option program. "With the stock program, your job stops being a paycheck, and starts being the equity you are building into your family's future," said Rich McKenna, an executive vice president of Gallagher Bassett.

The decade of the 1980s brought financial and management control without destroying the creative, hard-driving, entrepreneurial spirit that had formed Arthur J. Gallagher & Co. It helped provide capital for expansion, and it helped to position the company for the future.

The Gallaghers also began to take steps to ensure the company's future leadership. In 1987, Bob Gallagher had completed 25 years at the helm of AJGCo. He had taken over as president in 1963, when Jim Gallagher left to become president of Inland Life Insurance Co.

In 1961, AJGCo. opened a Life Insurance Department, under the direction of Warren G. Van der Voort Sr. Shortly after, the company formed Inland Life. Inland Life was a public company whose board members and backers included some of the most prominent names in Chicago business, most of them friends, associates and relatives of the Gallaghers.

The experience taught the Gallaghers some valuable lessons about running a public company and it established the relationship with Warren G. Van der Voort Sr.; in those ways, it was extremely valuable to the development of AJGCo. But ultimately, Inland Life did not perform as the Gallaghers hoped, and it was sold in 1972. Jim then returned to AJGCo. to handle mergers and acquisitions, but Bob continued as president and chief executive officer.

To plan for succession is difficult enough in any company, and it can be especially hard in a family company. But the Gallaghers were determined that their company would not self-destruct like so many others. There were several young executives whom Bob considered as he pondered the question of succession. But ultimately, he found his answer very close to home: John's eldest child, J. Patrick Gallagher Jr.

Patrick had been raised in the company, listening to his grandfather, his father and his uncles talk business around holiday dinner tables. His father often was called away from supper to deal with a client, and sometimes he took Patrick with him. From an early age, Patrick was fascinated by the work his family did, and his passion grew during the summer he worked at AJGCo. as a youngster, and later during his experiences in the internship program.

Bob was determined that his successor would understand and value the corporate culture that had developed at AJGCo., a culture that emphasized meeting the needs of both employees and clients. That culture was, in large part, the culture of the Gallagher family; as a member of that family, Patrick was part of that culture.

But it wasn't enough that the next generation of leadership understand the culture. The next head of the company also had to understand the business, and Patrick filled the bill there, too. He became a top salesman only a few years after joining the company, and he became one of its youngest unit managers just a few years after that.

Patrick's performance as a unit manager cemented Bob's belief that his nephew was the right choice. Patrick brought the concept of teamwork to the members of his unit, which included people both older and younger than himself. He gained the respect of his elders, and he guided and taught the younger people. In that way, he created a very successful unit in which both the culture and the business sides of the company developed and grew.

In 1985, when Patrick was only 33 years old, he was named to the newly created position of vice president of operations for the company, a move that made official Bob's choice of Patrick as the president in training. In 1990, Patrick became president and chief operating officer, and in 1995 he took over as CEO.

Once Bob decided to name Patrick as the next head of AJGCo., he focused on preparing Patrick. "Both Bob and my father were excellent mentors to me as I moved into top management," Patrick said. "At the same time, they were very comfortable with giving up power."

Inevitably, there were those who complained—both publicly and privately—about the ascension of Patrick. Bob listened to their objections and concerns, but he never wavered in his belief that Patrick was the right man for the job. Ultimately, some people left the company, convinced that their career paths had been blocked. Bob was sorry to lose good people, but he kept many more than he lost, and those who stayed have come to agree with the correctness of the choice.

Going public and the decision to make Patrick Gallagher the next head of AJGCo. were among the most important events of the 1980s for the company, but there were other milestones.

In 1980, AJGCo. started International Special Risk Services Inc., to provide Gallagher brokers with access to the domestic excess/surplus and reinsurance marketplace; today, ISRS is led by David McGurn.

In addition, the company introduced its RISX-FACS computer information system in 1983, and the system became a standard for online claims management. That same year, Joseph DeChristofaro was recruited to start Arthur J. Gallagher International Inc. to serve multinational clients.

In the middle of the decade, in 1985, Arthur J. Gallagher died at the age of 92, after a long life blessed with a happy marriage and loving and successful children. He had lived to see the company that he started grow and prosper, benefiting not only his family, but a much larger family of employees that had grown to almost 1,200 by the middle of the decade.

In the year Art Gallagher died, his company was chosen by Forbes magazine as one of the 200 Best Small Companies in America, an honor that it would receive three times.

In 1984, the company added its first outside directors: Jack M. Greenberg, chief financial officer of McDonald's Corp.; James Wimmer, senior partner in the Chicago law firm of Lord, Bissell & Brook; and Bob Baldwin, chairman of Morgan Stanley.

As the decade wound down, AJGCo. was becoming a much larger company: Revenues at AJGCo. reached $100 million in 1986, only a decade after the company first recorded $10 million. The following year, in 1987, revenues topped $134 million, there were more than 1,600 employees, and Business Month magazine named AJGCo. as one of the 200 fastest-growing companies in the country.

It was indeed a long way from the one-man operation that Art Gallagher started in 1927. Even then, though, Art had a faith in himself and a vision of what his company could be, and he had passed those to his sons. Now his grandson would become the guardian of that vision.

Chapter 9
An Expanding Family

"Mediocrity knows nothing higher than itself, but talent instantly recognizes genius."

Sherlock Holmes (Sir Arthur Conan Doyle)

Going public expanded the financial resources available to Arthur J. Gallagher & Co., and the company took advantage of that by working even harder to expand. • Much of the growth of Arthur J. Gallagher & Co. in the 1980s and beyond has come through a very successful and meticulously planned merger and acquisition program. The AJGCo. merger approach stresses a carefully reasoned strategy of identifying compatible agencies and creating a partnership with those agencies that benefits everyone. But the Gallaghers' first foray into acquisitions was a little less scientific. • In 1957, a well-known Chicago broker named Lloyd W. Hill died, and the Continental Bank became trustee of his estate, which included a personal lines book of business worth about $50,000. Jim, Bob and John Gallagher thought that this business would enhance their own. They put in a bid of $40,500 on the business, and their bid was accepted. • Art Gallagher was out of town when Lloyd W. Hill died and his book of business became available, and Art's sons made their own decision and acted on it. The next hurdle the brothers faced was telling their father about their purchase. Art had never spent that kind of money to acquire business, and the younger Gallaghers were not sure how he would react to the news. So they devised a plan.

At the time, Art was vacationing in the Caribbean with Leo J. Sheridan, a Chicago real estate developer and a close personal friend, who also was John's father-in-law. The brothers decided to wait until late afternoon to call Art. They would give him a chance to have a relaxing day in the sun, maybe enjoy a few cocktails, and then they would tell him about their bold move.

Their timing was good, and their phone connection was bad. Art was in a pleasant state of mind, and the static on the line made it difficult to give him more than the basic facts of the deal. When they hung up, they felt that Art had taken the news well. The next day, though, he landed in Miami on his way home, and he called the office. "He didn't even need a phone to make himself heard," John laughed.

The Lloyd W. Hill deal was the first Gallagher acquisition, but it was far from typical. Early on, the Gallaghers decided they were not interested in acquiring other people's problems. Instead, they wanted to create relationships with strong, effective operations that enhanced or expanded their own position in the marketplace.

When Jim returned to AJGCo. from Inland Life in 1972, he took over the mergers and acquisitions program. He had been exposed to a master of acquisition strategy in Bill Karnes, who served on the Inland Life board of directors and acted as the head of its acquisition committee. Karnes also was the chief executive of Beatrice, which still was one of AJGCo.'s biggest clients and which had built itself into a major U.S. company by following a carefully planned and executed path of acquiring companies that were good corporate fits.

Jim pursued the partnership strategy of acquisitions for about five years; at the end of that time, he left the active management of Arthur J. Gallagher & Co., although he remained an important and valued member of the board. During those five years, he completed several significant mergers, including the Mochel Agency in Downers Grove, Illinois; the Holt Agency in Dallas; and the Wightman Agency in St. Louis.

In 1985, Warren Van der Voort Jr. took over the task of guiding AJGCo. along the road of mergers and acquisitions. He was chosen specifically by Bob Gallagher for this position, and he was admirably suited for the role.

Van der Voort had joined the company in 1967, after going through the internship program. He had risen from an account executive to a top producer to a sales manager to the president of the Chicago Metro branch in Downers Grove. He was a professional broker, and his knowledge and experience gave him great credibility with potential merger partners.

When he took his new position in 1985, Van der Voort wrote a White Paper outlining Gallagher's corporate merger strategy that still is used to guide the merger effort. (At AJGCo., ideas that work are kept around; there is no updating for the sake of updating.)

The mission statement for the merger/acquisition team reads:

"Our long-range strategic plan and current business plan incorporates the goal of building a growing stream of pretax profits in new marketing areas through properly controlled and administered mergers and acquisitions.

"We are seeking mergers and acquisitions as an additional means to structure our national and international operations. We want to join forces with the kind of people and organizations where our linkage effectively uses resources and facilities to increase our rate of growth and profits. Acquisitions will be made to gain strong new people, new locations, new fields of insurance marketing or increase strength in existing areas."

AJGCo. develops a list of potential merger partners by identifying agencies in geographic or market areas in which AJGCo. would like to expand. The company is always on the lookout for smaller agencies that have distinguished themselves in some way. In many cases, these agencies are not for sale–but then, cold-calling is an honored tradition at AJGCo.

AJGCo. targets operations that have a history of success. In some cases, the potential merger partners represent strong competition to AJGCo. in a particular area; in other cases, they are located in an area where AJGCo. has no presence or a limited presence.

"We're not just trying to buy revenue and earnings, which is what most of our competitors have done–and failed at," Van der Voort said. "We're looking for organizations that we can partner with."

In addition to a company's business outlook, AJGCo. looks for companies that are a good philosophical fit. In fact, the Gallagher culture has become a strong selling point for the merger team.

"We're not the biggest, but we have what other people and organizations want," Van der Voort says. "Our merger partners have become the strongest spokesmen for our culture."

When the merger committee has identified potential candidates, AJGCo. representatives pay a call on the agency. The AJGCo. presentation stresses the idea of partnership. The smaller agency can strengthen AJGCo. in some way, and AJGCo. can offer it a nationally respected name, a variety of market strengths, and a strong and compassionate management style.

"We have no timetable, no forced deals," Van der Voort said. "We percolate on a pace that's comfortable for us and for them."

Sometimes the agency and AJGCo. will try a joint venture or a business deal to test their compatibility–"kind of like living together while you weigh whether to formalize the arrangement," Van der Voort said.

Among the first mergers after Van der Voort drew up his White Paper was with the Heffernan, Keiler & Doble agency in San Francisco. In 1986, when the merger was completed, the Heffernan agency was the largest independent insurance agency in San Francisco. The company had more than 100 employees and did about $9 million in annual revenues from its main office in San Francisco and its satellite office in Los Angeles.

Frank Heffernan, who owned the agency, had been in contact with the Gallaghers, off and on, for several years. During the 1970s, Jim Gallagher had called Heffernan and asked if he might be interested in a merger. Jim had heard about the Heffernan agency from insurance companies on the West Coast, and the AJGCo. brokers were familiar with Heffernan because the agency wrote a great deal of Catholic business.

Jim flew to San Francisco to talk to Heffernan, and then Heffernan traveled to Chicago. Heffernan was impressed by much of what he heard and saw, but the timing was not right for him. He had started the business not too many years before, and he was still a young man, eager for the challenge of seeing where he could take this young agency on his own.

By the early 1980s, he was ready to consider an offer. He actually sold his agency to another firm in 1984, but the agreement had an option to buy the business back. Heffernan exercised that option, because he just didn't feel right about the deal. Bob Gallagher got back in touch about that time, and Heffernan began negotiations with Bob and Mike Cloherty.

"One night in a restaurant bar at midnight, we struck a deal," Heffernan said. "It was a personal thing–I really liked Bob Gallagher."

There was more to it than that, of course. AJGCo. and the Heffernan agency were a perfect fit. In the spirit of the Gallagher merger philosophy, each brought something very valuable to the agreement.

The Heffernan agency provided AJGCo. with a major presence on the West Coast. In 1984, the agency's $9 million in annual revenues was five times the amount AJGCo. was doing at the time on the West Coast. Heffernan and his agency were well-known and well-respected in California, and they brought instant visibility and credibility to the new Gallagher Heffernan operation.

On the other hand, the Gallagher merger was a way for Heffernan, who was 55 at the time, to capitalize on his life's work. It also put the Heffernan agency into the company of big-league brokers, with a national and even international presence. And, it promised security for Heffernan's employees.

Heffernan was especially concerned that any merger not destroy the culture he had built at his agency, and a big part of the reason he agreed to the Gallagher merger was that he believed AJGCo. had a compatible culture. He was right.

"After the merger, my company remained the same–it just continued to grow," he said.

The potential of the Gallagher Heffernan merger has been more than realized in the past 10 years. In 1995, AJGCo. expected to do about $55 million in revenues on the West Coast. Frank Heffernan has become a point man for the company in arranging mergers in the region, and he calls on his own experience when evaluating potential partners.

Heffernan believes that the most important factors in his decision to accept Bob Gallagher's offer that night, and the most important reasons the merger has been a success, are the integrity and reputation of AJGCo. He believed what Bob Gallagher told him, and he has not been disappointed in that belief. In fact, he has advised against pursuing several potential West Coast merger partners since then because he felt they did not have the same commitment to dealing fairly and honestly with customers and employees.

Van der Voort believes that the Gallagher culture is one of the strongest selling points with merger partners. The cultural influence begins with the decision to seek strong, compatible companies rather than adopting a "Pac-Man" approach of chasing down and eating up weaker operations. The Gallagher organization is exceptionally entrepreneurial and people-focused, and it attracts other companies with a similar approach.

"The driving force of this company, promoted and nurtured by the Gallaghers, always has been a focus on people and their development," Van der Voort said. "It is our corporate culture to treat everyone almost like family; our merger partners are like extended family."

In the past decade, AJGCo. has extended its family through mergers with operations throughout the country and abroad. Mergers are explored and completed in all the areas that AJGCo. pursues, including brokerage, benefits, self-insurance administration and others. In each case, though, the same rigorous standards are applied to ensure a compatible and mutually beneficial fit.

Because of this highly selective and carefully reasoned approach to mergers, AJGCo. completes only a handful–about four to six–a year. The pace may pick up; increasingly, agencies are seeking out AJGCo. to discuss merger possibilities. And as the company continues to grow, of course, its resources and opportunities continue to expand.

But no one at AJGCo. expects the company to abandon its careful and considered approach to finding merger candidates. It continues to be vital to find merger partners that share AJGCo.'s beliefs and vision. Such companies are not easy to find. But, AJGCo. believes, they are worth the effort of the search.

Chapter 10
Avenues Of Growth

"No one knows what he can do till he tries."

Publilius Syrus, "Maxims"

In addition to the growth that has come through mergers and acquisitions, Arthur J. Gallagher & Co. has experienced significant internal growth. In all its areas of expertise, the company has expanded both its opportunities and its revenues. • The brokerage business, the core business of AJGCo., always has supplied a steady and reliable revenue stream, even when the industry in general has faltered. AJGCo. acted to strengthen the brokerage business in the late 1970s, with the formation of the branch office system under the direction of Walt McClure. • McClure came to AJGCo. in September 1976, as a unit manager. After a few years, Bob asked him to become vice president of branch operations. At that time, there were a handful of AJGCo. offices around the country–Chicago, St. Louis, Dallas, Los Angeles, Denver, Miami. Walt was charged with the task of pulling those branches together as a group, and of continuing to grow the branch network. • As the company grew, McClure continued to be the main–and sometimes the only–link between the branches and the corporate headquarters. He worked with merger partners who became branches, and with AJGCo. people sent out to open new scratch branches, and he helped to mold them all into a cohesive, integrated and professional brokerage sales force dedicated to the AJGCo. sales philosophy.

In 1986, the company regionalized the brokerage system, dividing the branches into Western, Central and Eastern divisions, and in 1993, AJGCo. created the Brokerage Services Division, with McClure as chairman and Gary Van der Voort as president. Before taking this new position, Gary Van der Voort had used the intelligence and intensely competitive spirit he displayed as a champion gymnast at the University of Michigan to turn the fledgling Miami office into the top AJGCo. branch in the country.

The brokerage system was not the only avenue of growth for AJGCo., though. Gallagher Bassett always has been an important contributor, and it became even more valuable to clients and to the company with the development of the RISX-FACS system, which revolutionized claims administration and put GB in a technological class by itself. RISX-FACS was the result of a longtime commitment by AJGCo. to technology–a commitment that started when a computer barely fit in a room and no one even dreamed of the day when one would fit in a briefcase.

Computerization was especially important to Gallagher Bassett because of the claims-handling requirements involved in self-insurance. In the beginning of GB, before there were any real commercial applications for computers, all the statistical work of administering claims was done by hand, using a hand-operated calculator that Sterling had taken with him from Western Adjustment. But as computerization became more available to American businesses, Sterling recognized the value of using computer data bases, not only to handle claims, but also to design and promote loss prevention efforts. The idea was to enter claims data and use that data to determine patterns that then could be used to set up loss control efforts.

One of the first examples of the value of this idea came when Beatrice acquired a candy company in Chicago. The candy company had an unusual number of workers compensation claims, and Gallagher Bassett could not figure out why. Then GB began to analyze the claims data and discovered that about 80 percent of the claims were occurring on the night shift.

Gallagher Bassett sent a safety engineer to the plant during the night shift, and he found that most of the night-shift workers spoke mainly or exclusively Spanish. Therefore, they didn't understand the posted safety regulations and instructions, which were in English. The GB safety engineer suggested that the safety materials be printed in both English and Spanish; when the company implemented bilingual communications, the number of injuries–and claims–at night fell dramatically. It was a textbook lesson in the value of loss prevention, in both financial and human terms.

"That's exactly what Gallagher Bassett was set up to do; that was our goal," Sterling said.

At first, Gallagher Bassett farmed out its computer needs to companies that specialized in computer services. Eventually, however, the company decided that it would be more efficient to take over the computer work itself.

Gallagher Bassett, and AJGCo., went through several false starts trying to build a system that would meet their needs. In 1980, AJGCo. hired Rich Kieffer, who had developed the reservations computer system for United Airlines, and assigned him the task of designing and setting up a computer system that would meet the needs of Gallagher Bassett and its growing list of clients. Kieffer determined that the whole existing system would have to be torn down, and he would have to start from scratch.

The process of building the new system was difficult and lengthy. But when the system, called RISX-FACS, finally was introduced in 1983, it revolutionized the claims administration industry. It was an online, real-time risk management information system with enormous capacity, and it provided Gallagher Bassett and GB clients with immediate, accurate and extensive information. RISX-FACS remains one of the most important assets of Gallagher Bassett, and other software products and services have been added that build on the RISX-FACS foundation and help Gallagher Bassett maintain the technological dominance that it established with RISX-FACS.

At the same time RISX-FACS was making its debut, the insurance market was undergoing a serious contraction in the availability of coverage, especially in many casualty lines. Traditionally the insurance industry has been subject to hard and soft cycles, in which coverage is alternately costly and difficult to obtain, and then less expensive and readily available. In a soft market cycle, coverage costs drop and the amount and types of coverage expand, creating a situation that is beneficial for buyers. Eventually, though, insurers decide they no longer can afford to sell their products at those low prices, and a hard market cycle begins.

In the early 1980s, though, a phenomenon occurred that far outstripped the usual market cycles. Insurers were reeling under huge liability claims in areas such as asbestos damage and pharmaceutical liability; to make matters worse, many of these claims were being filed years or even decades after insurers had sold the coverage under which the claims were filed. This meant that the premium the insurers had received was dramatically out of sync with the claims they were having to pay. The industry fought back by raising prices dramatically and rewriting policies to restrict severely or to eliminate entirely their liability in some areas.

Corporations large and small, as well as municipalities and government entities, began to see their liability coverage dry up and disappear. Towns removed diving boards from public pools, altered playground equipment in parks, and dropped sports programs in a desperate, and often futile, attempt to find coverage at an affordable price–and later to find coverage at all.

Corporations also saw their rates rise dramatically and the extent of their coverage begin to erode substantially, especially in areas like product liability, directors and officers, errors and omissions and other liability lines. In the light of this insurance crisis, self-insurance became not only the best alternative–it became, often, the only alternative.

As a creator of and the dominant company in the alternative market, AJGCo. found its expertise and the services of Gallagher Bassett in increasing demand. Armed with its new information system, which exponentially increased its claims-handling capabilities and made it possible to serve virtually any client, no matter how large or far-flung, GB was in an enviable position in which the demand for its products taxed the ability of the sales force to keep up.

"When the customers want brooms, you go out and get more brooms to sell," said Patrick Gallagher. And Gallagher Bassett was ready to sell brooms.

At that time, Gallagher Bassett services were sold exclusively by AJGCo. brokers, as part of a complete coverage package. The decision to keep GB captive to AJGCo. had been made early on, by Bob and Sterling, as a way of keeping GB's costs down and of giving the AJGCo. brokers a powerful sales tool. The coverage spasm in the market, however, created an enormous demand for GB from clients and from competing brokers alike.

After much discussion, Bob and Patrick decided the time had come to let GB move out on its own. The move was made in three steps: First, GB services could be sold exclusive of insurance, on a stand-alone basis, but still only by AJGCo. brokers. Next, GB hired its own sales force and made sales on its own. Finally, GB was allowed to deal with other brokers, and directly with insurers.

The independence of Gallagher Bassett, which was completed in 1988, was a very difficult decision. To lead GB into this new era, Bob and Patrick chose Peter Durkalski. Durkalski was no stranger to challenges: He came to AJGCo. in 1973 through the internship program and became the top new-business producer in the country in 1979. He was named a unit manager and later spearheaded a turn-around of the troubled International Special Risk Services division.

Throughout his career at AJGCo., Durkalski had used his engineering back-ground and intelligent tenacity to define tough problems and to find solutions. But when he was named president of GB in 1988, Durkalski faced his toughest problem yet: how to build GB into a separate company.

First, there were the challenges of setting up financial controls and organiza-tional charts. Under the direction of Jack Lazzaro, the chief financial officer of Gallagher Bassett, the company reorganized into profit centers and established more financial accountability for individual areas.

And there was the challenge of dealing with the shock that an independent GB created within AJGCo. The unbundling of GB provoked understandable resentment among the AJGCo. brokers, who suddenly found themselves without exclusive access to one of the most powerful weapons in their arsenal. Bob stuck by his guns, however. He met with AJGCo. brokers to explain the wisdom of the decision and how it was the right move for the company. He tried hard to win their support, and in most cases he was successful. But even when he encountered impassioned opposition, he remained convinced that unbundling GB was the right thing to do, and that everyone was just going to have to live with it.

Gallagher Bassett seized the opportunities presented by the hard market, RISX-FACS and its internal changes, and capitalized on those opportunities. At the end of 1988, Gallagher Bassett was doing $37 million in revenues and only about 5 percent of its business came from outside Arthur J. Gallagher & Co. At the end of 1994, GB was at $97 million in revenues, and more than 70 percent of that came from GB's own sales force or from outside brokers, rather than from AJGCo.

The company has expanded at both ends of the corporate spectrum as well. The technological capabilities of RISX-FACS allowed GB to increase its customer base among the largest U.S. corporations. At the same time, AJGCo. has expanded the pooling concept it developed for municipalities and applied it to the corporate market as well, giving even small companies the opportunity to realize the benefits of self-insurance–and the need for the services of Gallagher Bassett.

Despite the changes, however, there is much about Gallagher Bassett that remains essentially the same.

"We have always had a very common-sense approach to running the company, and Sterling was the first to take that approach," Durkalski said. "The common thread running throughout the history of this company is a commitment to juggling sales, profits and the entrepreneurial spirit of the sales force."

Other areas of AJGCo. also have experienced impressive growth over the past decade, fueled by the same common sense and commitment. AJGCo.'s employee benefits business started under Warren Van der Voort Sr., who headed the effort to sell mass-marketed life, auto and homeowners coverages on a payroll-deduct basis. By the mid-1970s, AJGCo. decided it needed a formal benefits effort, and the company formed the Group Department. Jim Durkin joined this department in 1976.

The company as a whole was growing very rapidly during the '70s. "In the late 1970s, every day you'd walk down the hall and meet a few new people we'd hired," Durkin said. The Group Department also was exploding; AJGCo. wrote its first self-insured benefits client in 1975, and by 1985, it had more than 120,000 covered lives.

However, both at AJGCo. in general and in the benefits division, the growth was almost out of control. As part of the move toward professional management, AJGCo. was reorganized in 1985 along product lines, and strict financial accountability standards were established. At that time, Durkin was named vice president of Gallagher Benefit Services. It was a dubious honor–in 1986, the division did only $8 million in revenues and had a loss of $1.5 million.

Most of the loss was related to problems with converting to a new computer system. At one point in 1986, the benefits division was working under three separate systems: a manual system, in which claims were entered via punch cards; the computer system that was being replaced; and the new system.

Once the computer problems were worked out, Durkin and his team turned their attention to developing their business. First, they discovered that they actually were losing money on some business, and they increased their fees to many of their clients. They also expanded efforts in the areas of consulting and brokerage, in addition to the third-party administration (TPA) business of self-insurance. In 1986, 50 percent of the division's revenues came from TPA fees; today, TPA fees account for only about 30 percent, and the rest comes from the more profitable consulting and brokerage operations.

The budget the division put together at the beginning of 1987 showed them breaking even for the year; about halfway through that year, it became obvious that they were going to show a profit. "We've never looked back," Durkin said. In 1995, the division expected to realize approximately $10 million in pretax profit on approximately $50 million in revenues.

And it continues to grow and to expand its niches. The division always has been strong in the traditional insured benefits, such as group life, health, dental and disability coverages. But recent mergers have expanded its expertise into actuarial services and retirement planning.

The benefits operation, and all the other parts of Arthur J. Gallagher & Co., work together to serve all clients completely. "You must be able to meet all a client's needs, or someone else will," Durkin said.

Spurred by both its internal growth and its growth through mergers, Arthur J. Gallagher & Co. has continued on its path of impressive expansion. In 1984, the year that the company went public, AJGCo. reported $64,178,716 in revenues and more than $6 million in net earnings; there were 1,026 employees. A year later, the company had $81,572,343 in revenues, almost $10 million in earnings and 1,158 employees.

At the end of 1984, the company had tangible net worth of $22.8 million, and its revenue per-employee was $62,553. In 1994, a decade after going public, AJGCo. had tangible net worth of $89 million and per-employee revenue of $107,732. During that 10 years, the company repurchased $95 million of its shares and paid out $64 million in dividends. In 1994, AJGCo. reported more than $356 million in revenues and $34.5 million in earnings. There were 3,308 employees in 57 sales offices and 109 service offices in the United States and abroad.

1995 was a record-setting year for Arthur J. Gallagher & Co. But then, almost every year sets records at AJGCo. With very few missteps along the way, the company has continued to build its business and its bottom line, steadily and impressively, despite difficulties in the industry and the problems that accompany the change from a small brokerage to a global company.

The company has accomplished this growth through a combination of excellent products and services, strong management, and the hard work and commitment of its employees. And AJGCo. plans to continue to build, right into the next century and beyond.

Chapter 11
The Challenge Of The Future

"Culture itself is neither education nor lawmaking; it is an atmosphere and a heritage."

H.L. Mencken

In 1927, Art Gallagher set his sights on the moon and launched a company. • In 1995–68 years after its founding, 32 years after Bob Gallagher took over as president, 11 years after becoming a public company and the first year with Patrick Gallagher as CEO–Arthur J. Gallagher & Co. continued to set records for financial performance, and to set the standard for client service. • Once again in 1995, AJGCo. turned in an impressive performance in the listing of top companies, according to a ranking by Holt Value Associates. Holt, which does quantitative research for money managers, ranked AJGCo. first overall among financial companies of medium size in the Chicago Tribune's top 100 Chicago-area companies, and seventh out of 176 companies in this category nationwide. AJGCo. received an A in the category of stock market appraisal of management skills. In all the measures of its financial performance, AJGCo. was at or near the top in the Tribune list. • "We're a very, very powerful company financially, and we want to continue that and to build on it, because that is job security for everyone," Bob Gallagher said. AJGCo. has identified several areas for growth. First, of course, is just to keep doing what the company has done so well for decades–calling on customers. The methods have changed somewhat from the days when Art Gallagher went knocking on doors. Today's sales force uses fax machines and cellular phones, but the message is the same: Let us help you with your insurance and risk management needs.

The company also plans to continue growing through mergers and acquisitions. Since the merger program began in earnest in 1985, more than 30 agencies have joined their fortunes with AJGCo. These mergers increase the company's revenues, and they add to its expertise and to the family of knowledgeable and skilled professionals who represent AJGCo.'s philosophy of customer service.

The benefits area also is a strong candidate for growth. After accomplishing an impressive turnaround, AJGCo.'s benefits division is proceeding full steam ahead. The recent debate over health care reform, concerns about Baby Boomers' retirement security, and discussion about changing the tax treatment of employee benefits have created an atmosphere that is ripe for creative solutions, and AJGCo. has a history of providing such solutions.

Gallagher Bassett is expanding its product line and its sales force, and forging more and stronger relationships with clients, with the brokerage community and with insurance companies. GB continues to be one of the pre-eminent names in insurance services, and the demand for such services continues to rise.

In fact, the alternative market itself continues to grow and expand. During the insurance availability crisis of the early 1980s, companies flocked to the alternative market, which became for many the market of last resort. After the crisis eased, the pundits expected that clients would return to the traditional market.

However, the pundits were wrong. Insurance buyers made an important discovery during the insurance crisis, a discovery similar to that made by many baseball fans during the season-ending strike of 1994: They could get along just fine on their own. Insurance buyers had been burned by the traditional market, and they were in no hurry to put their hands on the stove again—especially since they found they didn't need to. Just as the Gallaghers and Sterling Bassett had foretold, buyers came to see that self-insurance and other non-traditional risk-transfer arrangements allow a client to exercise much greater control over its expenses, and over its risk management program. With a well-designed alternative market program, a client can pay less, get more, and improve safety in the bargain.

As one of the creators of the alternative market, AJGCo. benefits greatly from this trend. The company has claimed the alternative market as its special area of expertise, and is continually expanding its position. Recently, for example, AJGCo. launched a division to set up and service captive insurance companies.

Finally, AJGCo. plans to grow by expanding its horizons—significantly. In 1927 and for many years thereafter, AJGCo. was primarily a Chicago company. The success of the Bishop's Plan drew AJGCo. across the country, and now the company is ready to take on the world.

Under the leadership of John Gallagher, AJGCo. is exploring business options abroad. Current efforts focus on English-speaking countries, especially the United Kingdom, but AJGCo. expects to break the language barrier one day, too.

Much of the future growth of AJGCo. will come from each area of the company pursuing business on its own, capitalizing on its own strengths. A decade ago, the three major business lines—brokerage, benefits and GB—shared most of their accounts. An AJGCo. broker would contact a client and sell that client a self-insurance plan that included some traditional coverage, benefits and the TPA services of Gallagher Bassett.

Accounts still are shared, of course, but increasingly the three business lines are pursuing clients on their own. With the unbundling of Gallagher Bassett and the growth of the benefits division, these two product lines have become strong, independent entities. The brokerage side, which remains AJGCo.'s top revenue-producer, also has developed more business independently. And all three areas plan to continue developing along these lines, as well as in concert with each other.

The exceptional growth that Arthur J. Gallagher & Co. has experienced and expects to experience creates great opportunities, but it also creates one of the most important challenges the company will face as it heads toward the next century: maintaining its corporate culture.

At many companies, the idea of a corporate culture is a misnomer–hostile takeovers, layoffs and management changes have destroyed any semblance of a set of guiding principles.

At AJGCo., though, there have been no hostile takeovers, and the chairman has been part of the company literally since birth. This company has developed a culture of shared values and expectations, and it is committed to keeping that culture alive.

"The Gallagher culture is very important–if we lose it, we become just another company," said Joe Fahey, corporate vice president in the Chicago Metro office.

That culture reflects the fact that, in the beginning, AJGCo. was a family company. Its values were family values, before that became a political buzzword.

Family remains important at AJGCo.; the company is sprinkled with Gallaghers, Van der Voorts and other familiar names. Parents are pleased and proud to see their children want to follow them into the company, and the company is pleased and proud to welcome them. Bob Gallagher says often, and without apology, "We believe in nepotism; it has always worked for us."

But AJGCo. has grown into a multinational, multimillion-dollar business with thousands of employees. The challenge will be maintaining those founding values because "now we're a much bigger family," said Florence Craig, who joined the AJGCo. family in 1951.

The AJGCo. family values include honesty and integrity, the will to win, chutzpah (or the Irish equivalent), and an abiding compassion and concern for people.

In a very real sense, Art Gallagher broke away from Moore Case Lyman & Hubbard because he felt it was dishonest of them to pay him less than his more high-brow colleagues. This commitment to honesty and to treating people fairly never has fallen into disfavor at Arthur J. Gallagher & Co., as it has at many other firms.

"I have never been lied to at this company," Joe Fahey said simply. Fahey joined AJGCo. in 1971 and, in all those years, "I haven't always heard just what I wanted to hear, but I have never been lied to."

The company also never has backed down from a challenge. From the very start, there was nothing the Gallaghers thought they could not do. "We were talking about major moves when we didn't have $1 million in revenues," Bob laughed. Now they have more than $400 million in revenues, they have made most of those moves successfully, and they are looking to make more.

The key to this confidence is the company's sales expertise. AJGCo. is a highly competitive, entrepreneurial, sales-focused company. It is no accident that many AJGCo. managers were athletes in high school or college.

"We have a lot of people who like to win, who hate to lose," said Gary Van der Voort. "People take losses personally, feeling as if the other guy outworked them. These are the people who succeed in this company."

The competitive attitude extends only to the competition, however. Within Arthur J. Gallagher & Co., there is remarkably little of the backstabbing and undercutting that characterize the climb up many corporate ladders.

"Our people tend to get along with each other, they tend to look for ways to help each other," said Bill Jensen, a senior vice president who joined the company in 1971.

Indeed, consideration for people and their needs, especially the people who make up Arthur J. Gallagher & Co., is the pre-eminent family value. James Wimmer said, "I've practiced corporate law for 45 years, and I think this is really unique. People really care about people in this organization."

People are allowed to make mistakes, to try and fail. Jim Keough, who is the area president for the Chicago Metro region, recalled being a young producer shortly after he joined the company in 1967. He had been working hard on a big sale and he really thought he had it, when the customer called up and told him the deal was off. Keough was devastated; it was his first major failure, and he felt terrible about it. On top of it all, he had to go directly from that phone call to a sales meeting in Bob Gallagher's office.

In those days, the whole staff fit into Bob's office and, after everyone had gathered, Bob noticed that his young salesman seemed especially glum. He asked Keough if something was wrong and, after considerable hemming and hawing, Keough told Bob how he had lost the sale.

Bob turned to Dan Wachs, the first employee of AJGCo. and one of its most successful and respected salesman. "Dan," he said, "tell Jim about the first big sale you lost."

"That afternoon I realized that people don't need managers so much when things are going well," Keough said. "The manager's real importance comes when the wheels are falling off."

Loyalty to employees is a hallmark of AJGCo., and it is returned many times. There is remarkably little turnover among the company's managers. Although its top management averages less than 45 years of age, many of those people have been with the company for all or most of their careers.

"Bob made us all believers; he's a good salesman," said Walt McClure. "Arthur J. Gallagher & Co. is a bright star in a sky of broken operations and rudderless ships."

In May 1984, a month before the company went public, Bob Gallagher wrote down the ideas that provide the rudder for AJGCo. Rosemarie Martin, Bob's assistant at the time, said, "He just sat down and wrote it; he made very few changes to what he originally wrote. It came from his head and from his heart."

That document outlines the defining principles of Arthur J. Gallagher & Co. It explains what makes Arthur J. Gallagher & Co. unique, and the qualities from which the company draws its strength. It is still the company's guide, more than a decade after Bob Gallagher wrote from his heart, and Bob believes it will guide the company decades from now. It is called simply: The Gallagher Way

The Gallagher Way

Shared values at AJGCo. are the rock foundation of the Company and our Culture. What is a Shared Value? These are concepts that the vast majority of the movers and shakers in the Company passionately adhere to. What are some of AJGCo.'s Shared Values?

1. We are a **Sales & Marketing Company** dedicated to providing excellence in **Risk Management Services** to our clients.

2. We support one another. We believe in one another. We acknowledge and respect the ability of one another.

3. We push for professional excellence.

4. We can all improve and learn from one another.

5. There are no second-class citizens—everyone is important and everyone's job is important.

6. We're an open society.

7. Empathy for the other guy is not a weakness.

8. Suspicion breeds more suspicion. To trust and be trusted is vital.

9. Leaders need followers. How leaders treat followers has a direct impact on the effectiveness of the leader.

10. Interpersonal business relationships should be built.

11. We all need one another. We are all cogs in a wheel.

12. No department or person is an island.

13. Professional courtesy is expected.

14. Never ask someone to do something you wouldn't do yourself.

15. I consider myself support for our Sales & Marketing. We can't make things happen without each other. We are a team.

16. Loyalty and respect are earned—not dictated.

17. Fear is a turn-off.

18. People skills are very important at AJGCo.

19. We're a very competitive and aggressive Company.

20. We run to problems—not away from them.

21. We adhere to the highest standards of moral and ethical behavior.

22. People work harder and are more effective when they're turned on–not turned off.

23. We are a warm, close Company. This is a strength–not a weakness.

24. We must continue building a professional Company–together–as a team.

25. Shared values can be altered with circumstances–but carefully and with tact and consideration for one another's needs.

When accepted Shared Values are changed or challenged, the emotional impact and negative feelings can damage the Company.

Robert E. Gallagher, May 1984

Growth History

For more than three decades, Arthur J. Gallagher & Co. has seen its revenues increase by more than $400 million, earnings jump by more than $41 million, and employees increase from 19 to more than 3,700. The Company has accomplished this phenomenal growth because of its innovative approach to risk transfer and risk management, its unwavering commitment to customer service, and its entrepreneurial and people-centered corporate culture. Arthur J. Gallagher & Co. is confident that it can continue on this course into the 21st century, because creativity, hard work and commitment to people always will be the most important assets a company can offer its clients and its employees.

Note: *The figures in the accompanying chart show results since 1963, the first year for which comprehensive figures are available. The numbers are "as reported" and have not been restated for poolings of interests.*

Year	Revenues	Net Earnings	Employees	Per Capita Revenues
1963	$562,000	$(10,000)	19	$29,579
1964	583,000	14,000	22	26,500
1965	722,000	16,000	31	23,290
1966	863,000	20,000	37	23,324
1967	994,000	8,000	43	23,116
1968	1,215,000	58,000	51	23,824
1969	1,452,000	42,000	63	23,048
1970	2,026,000	98,000	83	24,410
1971	2,787,000	154,000	115	24,235
1972	3,493,000	175,000	141	24,773
1973	4,933,000	252,000	181	27,254
1974	6,130,000	372,000	200	30,650
1975	8,870,000	711,000	264	33,598
1976	12,075,000	1,085,000	324	37,269
1977	18,367,000	1,767,000	445	41,274
1978	24,817,000	2,558,000	553	44,877
1979	30,524,000	2,906,000	682	44,757
1980	37,535,000	3,008,000	822	45,663
1981	42,536,000	1,326,000	897	47,420
1982	48,477,000	3,217,000	893	54,286
1983	53,358,000	4,269,000	956	55,814
1984	64,179,000	6,296,000	1,026	62,553
1985	81,572,000	9,880,000	1,158	70,442
1986	118,845,000	15,405,000	1,465	81,123
1987	134,656,000	16,208,000	1,628	82,713
1988	156,035,000	16,895,000	1,766	88,355

Year	Revenues	Net Earnings	Employees	Per Capita Revenues
1989	173,206,000	17,254,000	1,900	91,161
1990	198,176,000	17,691,000	2,044	96,955
1991	231,679,000	18,790,000	2,341	98,966
1992	272,725,000	23,470,000	2,661	102,490
1993	317,663,000	32,271,000	2,975	106,777
1994	356,377,000	34,540,000	3,308	107,732
1995	$411,998,000	$41,491,000	3,739	$110,189

Volume II

John P. Gallagher/1927–1996/Vice Chairman, Arthur J. Gallagher & Co.

Prologue

We published The Gallagher Way in 1996 to chronicle the development of our company. We were proud of our success and confident about our future. And our confidence has been well-founded, as Arthur J. Gallagher & Co. has become the third-largest U.S. broker, and the fourth-largest broker in the world.

AJGCo. recorded this tremendous growth—and expects to continue to grow—by sticking to its plan. While some companies were consumed in a frenzy of mega-mergers, and other companies struggled to assimilate businesses they had consumed, Arthur J. Gallagher & Co. continued to emphasize the qualities that had always set it apart: hard work, market expertise and, above all, client satisfaction. By continuing to focus its efforts on serving clients and building business, the company navigated some turbulent times in our industry, the economy and the world, and emerged larger, stronger and more successful.

In addition, Arthur J. Gallagher & Co. has maintained its unique corporate culture, a culture built on respect for clients, respect for employees and respect for the value of teamwork. This culture was formed early, when Arthur J. Gallagher & Co. was really only Arthur J. Gallagher himself. It grew with the company, and it continues to be its cornerstone.

We decided to update The Gallagher Way after the company recorded the twin benchmarks of $1 billion in gross revenues and 75 years in business. The first volume remains unchanged, because we believe it accurately reflects the company as it grew until 1995. This new volume outlines the company as it has become, and continues becoming. We think you will find that, while much has changed, much has remained the same.

Unfortunately, one change has been the loss of one of the company's most influential leaders. On February 23, 1996, John P. Gallagher passed away. He was an inspiration to everyone who knew him. He is much missed, and this new volume is dedicated to his memory.

Robert E. Gallagher

J. Patrick Galligher Jr.

Chapter 12
Boiling And Roiling

"Vision is the art of seeing things invisible."

Jonathan Swift

In the closing decades of the 20th century, Arthur J. Gallagher & Co. was transforming itself from a smaller broker to a company that would be among the dominant insurance brokerages in the new century. • Many changes occurred in the industry and at AJGCo. during the 1980s. Among the most important was taking the company public. Arthur J. Gallagher & Co. stock was first offered on the NASDAQ on June 4, 1984, and the company joined the New York Stock Exchange in 1987. The original stock price in 1984 was $13.75 per share, which is $1.72 per share when adjusted for three 2-for-1 stock splits. By 1995, the value of that stock had risen 442 percent. At December 31, 2003, it was $32.49, or 1,788 percent higher than the adjusted original price. • Going public helped to provide liquidity for capitalizing insiders' life work, a public stock for mergers and capital for expansion. At the same time, Arthur J. Gallagher & Co. was putting in place a structure to help guide it as it grew. In 1985, Gallagher Benefit Services was established as a separate entity to handle the burgeoning benefits business. In 1986, the company organized its brokerage offices into regions. In 1988, it completed the unbundling of Gallagher Bassett, which allowed the explosion of growth that GB would experience over the coming decades.

Arthur J. Gallagher & Co. was quickly becoming a major brokerage company. Its revenues reached $100 million in 1986. A year later, in 1987, revenues topped $134 million, and Business Month magazine named AJGCo. one of the 200 fastest-growing companies in the nation.

Despite this success, AJGCo. was still seen by some in the industry as a specialized broker. J. Patrick Gallagher, chief executive officer, remembers manning a booth at the 1990 conference of the Risk & Insurance Management Society, the top conference in the industry. "No one came," Pat laughs. "Our reputation was, 'You guys are the guys who do churches and schools.'" In contrast, during the 2003 RIMS conference, the company sponsored an event at Chicago's Field Museum of Natural History, and 1,500 guests attended.

The start of the 1990s saw explosive growth for Arthur J. Gallagher & Co. In 1990, the company had revenues of $198 million, and by 1995 that had more than doubled, to almost $412 million. By 1995, Arthur J. Gallagher & Co. was ranked as the ninth-largest broker in the world in the annual ranking by Business Insurance magazine. Pat says, "By 1995, we knew we were good."

Pat notes that AJGCo.'s growth continued to be driven by the factors that had always fueled it. The company grew organically, adding more salespeople and selling more business. From the very beginning, AJGCo. had a strong sales orientation. Art Gallagher had been a consummate salesman–a friend once said that, "He had a thick pair of soles and a ball-bearing tongue." As his sons Jim, Bob and

John entered the business, they continued to refer proudly to themselves as "peddlers."

"The old-fashioned producer is alive and well at Gallagher," says Sam Babington, who heads the Mergers and Acquisitions Niche for the Brokerage Services Retail Division. "Our identity is very, very strong. We're a production-oriented company....We want people with very high integrity, very focused on accomplishing goals."

The old-fashioned producer was challenged in accomplishing those goals during the middle part of the decade. Although the insurance industry was stagnant in the mid-1990s, mired in a soft market, Arthur J. Gallagher & Co. continued its steady growth, often outpacing the industry as a whole.

But it was not easy. Pat Gallagher recalls that 1996 was a particularly difficult year. On February 23, 1996, John Gallagher died suddenly, leaving the company reeling. He had been an inspirational leader and a critical part of the company's growth from a local broker to an international force. Before his death, he had been deeply involved in Gallagher's efforts to expand in London and elsewhere abroad. His loss was especially hard on his son Pat and his brother Bob, AJGCo.'s chairman.

Revenues increased only 11 percent in 1996, and a mere 7 percent in 1997. Although this was a good showing in a very tough market, it was well below the company's average of 17 percent a year. Still, the company continued to believe in itself and in what it was doing.

"What I'm really proud of as a company is that we never made excuses for ourselves," Pat says. Management simply dug in their heels and did what they needed to do. Three times during the 1990s, the company froze salaries for people making more than $50,000 a year. During those wage freezes, Pat says, "We never lost a person." Gallagher employees understood the need to make personal sacrifices to help the company, and they believed that the hard times would end.

There was no panic at AJGCo. Instead, the company continued to follow its game plan, building business through organic growth and also through mergers and carefully selected acquisitions, which brought expansion in areas of expertise and geographic reach, as well as in number of employees.

In 1985, Bob Gallagher had put Warren Van der Voort Jr. in charge of guiding AJGCo. as it looked for merger partners. One of Van der Voort's first moves was to write a White Paper outlining the company's merger strategy. In part, it said, "We want to join forces with the kind of people and organizations where our linkage effectively uses resources and facilities to increase our rate of growth and profits. Acquisitions will be made to gain strong new people, new locations, new fields of insurance marketing or increase strength in existing areas."

AJGCo.'s management understood the need to find merger partners that were a good fit. They looked for partners that could enhance the company's business positions. And they looked for partners that had compatible cultures. This was a very different approach than that taken by much of the insurance industry. The late 1990s was a period of what Pat Gallagher calls "a boiling and roiling" in the industry, as major mergers and acquisitions redrew the list of the world's top brokers.

"There aren't many industries as goofy as ours," Bob Gallagher is fond of saying, and the latter years of the 20th century were goofy indeed.

In 1995, Arthur J. Gallagher & Co. was ranked as the ninth-largest broker in the world in the annual Business Insurance listing of top brokers. Four years later, in 1999, it was the fourth-largest broker in the world and, as Pat says, "We didn't pass anybody." Instead, the larger brokers were acquired by other firms in a frenzy of merger mania.

In 1996, Johnson & Higgins was ranked sixth and David A. Olsen, its chairman and CEO, told Business Insurance, "There's no question that we are not for sale." In 1997, Marsh & McLennan bought J&H for $1.8 billion. The following year, Marsh bought The Sedgwick Group.

Aon Corporation, which had bought Frank B. Hall in 1992, acquired Bain Hogg Group in 1996 and picked up Alexander & Alexander Services and The Minet Group in 1997. When the dust settled, Arthur J. Gallagher was ranked fourth, behind Marsh, Aon and Willis Group Holdings Ltd., a British broker. Among U.S.-based brokers, it was third, and it retains those rankings today.

Pat says that AJGCo. considered taking part in the merger mania, and even held discussions with some companies. But in the end, he says, "We stuck to what we knew. We stuck to our knitting."

AJGCo. looked at the newly defined brokerage world, and saw an important place for itself in that world.

After the mega-mergers, the top two brokers had become enormous companies–as they remain today. In 2002, Marsh reported $10.4 billion in revenues, while Aon had $8.8 billion. In contrast, Willis had $1.8 billion, and AJGCo. had slightly more than $1 billion.

But, AJGCo. had something the larger brokers did not have: an intact culture. The coming together of huge brokerage companies created a sort of Clash of the Titans. The newly merged companies had to integrate services, locations and people, including upper management. The result was unsettling.

Often the companies being acquired had cultures that were very different from the culture of the acquiring company. Where one was entrepreneurial, the other was more rigid. Even under the best of circumstances, creating huge companies required a culture to become more highly structured. As departments were consolidated, professionals found themselves in new positions, doing new jobs and answering to new bosses. And some of them did not like it.

Clients also had to cope with the changes. Clients that had dealt with one company for many years suddenly found themselves dealing with another one. The people who had represented them sometimes were no longer with the new company. Procedures changed, and there was no familiar voice on the other end of the phone. Although there were some advantages to being served by a new, larger company, there were many changes as well. And some clients did not like it.

"The customer wants choice," Pat Gallagher says. "And choice was being taken out of the market by the consolidation of the big companies."

AJGCo. could offer customers the choice they wanted, Pat believed. It could be an alternative to the mega-companies, offering the kind of client focus that had always been its trademark. And, he thought, AJGCo. could also be an alternative for some of the talented professionals who found themselves adrift in the wake of the mergers.

In other words, Arthur J. Gallagher would be what it had always been—a company that provided the best possible products and services to clients by employing the most talented people in the business and creating a culture that encouraged teamwork and hard work.

Tom Gallagher, president of Arthur J. Gallagher & Co. Risk Management Services Inc., says, "The strategy has always been to maintain the culture, make the hard calls and avoid the big mistake."

"Don't make the big mistake" became a mantra for the company, defined by Bob Gallagher as he watched the corporate and human fallout from the "culture-busting" mega-mergers. "We make little mistakes—you can fix those," he says. "That's an enormous advantage with us."

From the very beginning, Bob Gallagher had believed that the company is "divinely inspired. Good things happen to us." And Arthur J. Gallagher & Co. was prepared for good things as it staked a place at the top of the brokerage world.

Chapter 13
Thinking Outside The Box

"What would life be like if we had no courage to attempt anything?"

Vincent Van Gogh

The focus of Arthur J. Gallagher & Co. historically has been, and continues to be, insurance brokerage and risk management services. But the company never has been shy about thinking creatively to find ways to serve its clients–and add to its bottom line. From the start, when Art Gallagher helped to create the Retro Rating Program of the Hartford Group and devised the first large-deductible fire insurance policy for Bowman Dairy in the 1930s, the company he founded has been willing and able to think outside the box. • Many of those outside-the-box ideas have become part of the Specialty Marketing and International Division, headed by Dave McGurn. The division includes AJGCo.'s reinsurance, wholesale and excess/surplus brokerage operations in the United States and abroad, as well as captive management operations and risk management joint ventures. It also handles the wholesale e-commerce portal, CoverageFirst.com, which has more than 11,000 registered users among independent agents, wholesale brokers and managing general agents (MGAs).

The Specialty Marketing and International Division came into being in 1996. Before that, AJGCo. had done some business in these areas, but there was no separate entity. Creating the division allowed the company to launch an all-out effort to develop its specialty and international businesses, and that effort has paid off. In 1996, the division did $20 million in gross revenues and had $4 million in pretax profits. In 2003, it did $205 million in gross revenues and had $37 million in pretax profits.

The recent hard market, characterized by rising rates and shrinking coverages, has made the alternative market even more attractive for clients looking for cost-effective solutions to their insurance and risk management needs. The alternative market can be very challenging, and putting together coverages and handling programs requires experience and finesse. Much of the work of Arthur J. Gallagher & Co. is centered on helping companies find and manage coverage in the alternative market, and the Specialty Marketing and International Division has emerged at the front of the pack in helping clients navigate through these challenges.

The division was born, in part, in tragedy. John Gallagher had been handling the international interests of Arthur J. Gallagher & Co. He was very instrumental in setting up the company's first Lloyd's broker and in developing other business interests abroad. When he died in 1996, much of those responsibilities fell to Dave McGurn, who had been working closely with John, known as J.P. McGurn says, "J.P. was a mentor to me," and as McGurn has worked to build up the business of his division, he has been guided in no small part by his desire to help realize John's dreams.

When McGurn took over John's responsibilities, Joel Cavaness came from St. Louis to Gallagher headquarters in Itasca to head International Special Risk Services Inc. At the time, ISRS was basically an in-house wholesaler that dealt only with Gallagher offices. But McGurn and Cavaness realized that Gallagher retail brokers were still placing a lot of wholesale business with outside firms, and they knew that other brokers were also placing a lot of wholesale business. So they decided to go aggressively after that business.

On May 11, 1997, McGurn and Cavaness hired four people in Chicago to set up a wholesale brokerage operation. Joe Nelligan was the first employee. They, with the full support of the management of AJGCo., were taking an enormous leap of faith. "We didn't have a name, we didn't have any markets, we didn't have anything," Cavaness recalls. "We went out on a huge limb, out on the very tip."

Soon after, they hired an additional four people in Atlanta, headed by Jeff McNatt. Risk Placement Services (RPS) was born. The strategy was to find wholesale brokers that had existing relationships with Gallagher's retail brokers and convince them to come on board. "It all stems from relationships," McGurn says.

The experiment quickly began to pay off. Wholesalers signed on, and clients followed. "From that auspicious start," McGurn says, RPS has grown to 420 employees in 23 offices. In 2003, RPS generated $66 million in gross revenues.

RPS professionals do three different kinds of wholesale business. First, they conduct open brokerage, which is placing business for retail brokers that can't place the business on their own. This often involves dealing with hard-to-place markets or markets that require special capabilities. They also do a thriving MGA business, in which they underwrite on behalf of insurers that "subcontract" their underwriting to RPS because RPS has the necessary expertise. Finally, they have program management offices in Los Angeles and Washington state through which they handle programs from start to finish, including underwriting on behalf of the insurers. Usually these are large programs, such as public entity programs, that require specific understanding and experience that RPS brings to the table.

RPS, like its parent, has built its business through organic growth and through mergers. About 75 percent of its business is done with non-Gallagher brokers, allowing RPS not only to serve as an important resource for AJGCo. brokers but also to capture significant revenue from working with other brokers.

Like RPS, Risk Management Partners in the United Kingdom was a startup operation, in December 1994. "We started on Day One with absolutely no business on the books," says Kaz Janowicz, managing director of RMP. What they did have, though, were capabilities and talent that could fill a specific void in the U.K.

Those capabilities and talent were centered largely in Gallagher Bassett (UK), which was formed in 1990. But bringing Gallagher Bassett to the U.K. had begun about four years earlier, after Arthur J. Gallagher & Co. bought the Lloyd's broker John Plumer Ltd. Steve Prince, who was a broker for Plumer, was asked to do a feasibility study on whether Gallagher Bassett could be profitable in the U.K. The results of Prince's study were positive, and when John Gallagher and Jack Campbell offered him the chance to manage the first Gallagher Bassett office in the U.K., "I jumped at the chance," Prince says. Led by Prince and Russell Parsons, Gallagher Bassett's vice president of international operations, Gallagher Bassett (UK) has grown to 140 employees in seven offices. It is one of the largest third-party administrators in the United Kingdom, and the largest TPA specializing in public entities.

Much of its public entity business comes from RMP, and the success of RMP is due largely to Gallagher Bassett. "The fact that Gallagher Bassett was already in place in the U.K. made us ready when the opportunity to form Risk Management Partners came up," says Pat Gallagher.

Prior to 1993, Municipal Mutual Insurance Company Ltd. controlled almost all the public entity insurance business in the United Kingdom. But Municipal Mutual had inadequate rates and underwriting, and it went bankrupt. Zurich Insurance bought Municipal Mutual, and Zurich began to make changes, often raising rates and restricting coverages. Among other things, Zurich began writing coverage with very large deductibles, but it did not provide customers with the kind of extensive support and risk management information they needed to successfully manage large deductibles and self-insured retentions. Gallagher looked at the situation and realized there was an opportunity.

Arthur J. Gallagher & Co. created a joint venture with American Re in which American Re provided insurance coverage and Gallagher Bassett provided claims handling and risk management. "Risk Management Partners provided real competition to Zurich," Janowicz says. "We came in at the right time to provide a real alternative. And we have been a pain in their backside ever since."

The public entity market in England, Scotland and Wales was more than ready for RMP. Janowicz says that the expertise of Gallagher Bassett was an especially strong selling point. "Gallagher Bassett had very strong claims management experience and discipline. And it had Risx-Facs (Gallagher Bassett's Web-based claims and loss-control information management system), which was very innovative in the U.K. at the time," he says. "As a result, they created a very, very strong business here."

When RMP opened its doors, Zurich had about 90 percent of the public entity market. Now RMP has almost a quarter of that market, which includes municipalities, police and fire departments.

In January 2004, Arthur J. Gallagher & Co. took over full ownership of RMP. At the same time, American Re decided to concentrate on its U.S. business and AIG became the insurer for RMP clients. In 2003, RMP did about $70 million in written premiums.

McGurn is particularly proud of the way in which RMP has helped the company realize one of John Gallagher's dreams: to bring Gallagher Bassett to the U.K. "This was John's home run," McGurn says.

John Gallagher also was instrumental in setting up Gallagher operations in Bermuda, one of the centers of the alternative market. In 1975, John founded Arthur J. Gallagher (Bermuda), Ltd. As an important player in the alternative market, it was essential for Gallagher to have a presence in Bermuda, which has become the world's third-largest insurance marketplace.

"John Gallagher had always been an innovator, and Bermuda had long been the home of creative solutions," explains Jennifer Gallagher, John's daughter and the president of Innovative Risk Services (INRS), the marketing arm for Artex Insurance Company, Gallagher's Bermuda rent-a-captive facility.

Gallagher (Bermuda) operates as a wholesaler, providing entrance to the Bermuda market for both Gallagher and non-Gallagher retailers. The office, which is headed by David McManus, provides captive management, reinsurance placement and placement of individual risks in the Bermuda market. It also is the site of Artex Insurance Company.

Artex, established in 1997 in response to tightening in the insurance market, is the acronym for Alternative Risk Transfer Exchange. It is one of the largest property/casualty rent-a-captives in the world. Innovative Risk Services was created to be the U.S. sales and marketing arm for Artex, and also has developed its own proprietary workers compensation and medical malpractice products.

Bermuda adds significantly to the company's bottom line, sustaining double-digit growth for several years. It also is essential to AJGCo.'s "multiple bite" theory of growth, providing clients with many ways to serve their insurance needs. A presence in this market, like in London, is critical to Gallagher's continued growth as one of the elite companies in its industry.

Reinsurance also has become a major contributor to the bottom line of the Specialty Marketing and International Division. Gallagher made its first foray into reinsurance in the United States in 1987, when it bought E&S Intermediaries, a small firm based in New York. E&S was in financial trouble at the time of the acquisition, and joining with Arthur J. Gallagher & Co. gave E&S the credibility it needed to persuade ceding insurers to do business with it. Still, the reinsurance operation was fairly modest at the start. "We really were a small operation up until the early '90s," says Randy Jensen, who was with E&S at the time of the merger and who is now president of Arthur J. Gallagher Intermediaries.

Jensen took over the reinsurance operation in New York in 1995. During that year, the office did $2 million in revenues; in 2003, it did $11 million in gross revenues. Also during these years, additional offices were opened in Chicago, Los Angeles and Philadelphia.

In the early to mid-1990s, Gallagher began doing specialty treaty reinsurance business out of the New York office. Jensen says they looked at the clients of AJGCo.'s retail brokers for opportunities, and they found those opportunities in areas like pools, groups and alternative programs. "The business was really home-grown," Jensen says.

"I wasn't an expert," he adds. But he started bringing experts into the company, continuing a Gallagher tradition of providing opportunities for bright and ambitious young professionals. "At Gallagher, you have a lot of young people who aren't impeded toward their success because they're young. If you can sell, you can sell—it doesn't matter how old you are," Jensen says. "There are no impediments in this company to making money."

That specialty treaty business now accounts for about 45 percent of the revenues Arthur J. Gallagher Intermediaries generates. And, Jensen says, the development of that business exemplifies the Gallagher commitment to entrepreneurship. "At Gallagher, they like it when people develop an area of business," he says. "If you can show them that something will work, they are willing to commit the resources to build the infrastructure to make it work."

The development of the specialty treaty business involves many people and multiple resources, making the Gallagher culture of teamwork critical to its success. Jensen says, "Teamwork is huge in the culture. There is a lot of teamwork, and a minimal amount of politics."

The reinsurance business of Arthur J. Gallagher & Co. was expanded further with the August 2000 merger with John P. Woods Co. Inc. in Jersey City, N.J. The Woods agency now manages AJGCo.'s North American treaty reinsurance business. Jay Woods, president of John P. Woods Co. Inc., notes that having a reinsurance presence is very important as Arthur J. Gallagher & Co. continues its growth from a national to a global risk management company. "If you want to expand how we are known in the market, you have to have all the tools," he says.

The merger with the Woods agency is an example of how Gallagher builds business through mergers. Woods recalls that Bob Gallagher originally contacted his father in 1984 and said, "If you ever want to sell, let us know." The elder Woods was not interested in selling at the time, but he remembered the call.

More than a decade later, when Woods and his father decided to sell, it was in the aftermath of the merger mania that had gripped the world's largest brokers. They talked to many of those large brokers, Woods, says. But in the end, they decided to join forces with Gallagher.

The Gallagher culture was a good fit with the Woods culture, Woods says. Both placed a very high value on treating clients and employees fairly. Merging with Woods expanded Gallagher's presence in the important reinsurance market-place. And it gave the Woods agency a chance to become a player on a major stage.

"We wanted to be able to play in Yankee Stadium, and joining Gallagher gave us a uniform," Woods says.

Chapter 14
Going To London Town

"London is a roost for every bird."

Benjamin Disraeli

John Stancik first went to London in January 1990, to head Gallagher Plumer Ltd., Arthur J. Gallagher & Co.'s Lloyd's broker. Stancik, who now heads the Brokerage Services Retail Division's Northeast Region, spent the 1990s expanding the Gallagher presence in London. He enjoyed the history of the city, and especially its insurance business. London, home of the venerable Lloyd's of London, is one of the most important cities in the global insurance world. • "London has transacted insurance business worldwide for more than 300 years," explains Philip Nastri, the deputy managing director of Gallagher's current London operation. The London market is centered around Lloyd's of London, one of the longest-operating and most famous insurance underwriting organizations in the world. • Lloyd's is named after Edward Lloyd, who had a coffee shop in London in the late 1600s. He made a point of posting the latest shipping information, and many marine merchants and sea captains frequented his shop. His customers began to transact basic insurance underwriting there, agreeing to take part of each other's risk. In the early 1770s, a group of customers of the coffeehouse formed their own underwriting association, which became Lloyd's of London.

Lloyd's is among the world's leading markets for many traditional risks, especially marine and aviation insurance. It is also a major market for specialty coverages, and in fact much of its fame outside the industry revolves around the bizarre coverages Lloyd's has underwritten. For example, it has insured a grain of rice bearing a portrait of Queen Elizabeth II and Prince Philip. When Cutty Sark whisky offered a prize of 1 million pounds to anyone who could capture the Loch Ness monster alive, the company took out a policy with Lloyd's in case someone actually brought in the beast. Lloyd's also has insured the taste buds of a food critic and the nose of a whisky distiller, as well as provided coverage to a comedy troupe in case anyone in the audience died laughing.

London's insurance market is contained in a one-square-mile area, and as a result, it is built on face-to-face transactions. Brokers usually walk into the underwriter's office carrying information about the risk, and if the underwriter is interested, he signs his name to provide all or part of the coverage.

This market was the focus of John Stancik's efforts. By the mid-1990s, it had become apparent that the Gallagher presence in London was not sufficient. Gallagher Plumer, which became Arthur J. Gallagher & Co. (UK) Ltd., was too small an operation to be much help in promoting the parent company as a worldwide broker. "I knew we either had to shut it down or beef it up," Stancik says.

In early 1995, he was involved in negotiations to buy a marine broker. But one day as he was driving to work, Stancik says, he had one of Bob Gallagher's "divine inspirations." "I thought, 'Why do I want to be in the marine business?'"

Stancik says. He decided that what he really wanted to do was expand the company's treaty reinsurance capabilities.

He became interested in a treaty reinsurance broker called Morgan, Read and Coleman, Ltd. Shortly before Christmas 1995, he and Brian King, one of the broker's principals, met for coffee. The meeting took place "in some obscure place, so no one would recognize us," Stancik says. The conversation was very preliminary, and they agreed to talk again after the holidays.

They did meet again, and Stancik grew enthusiastic about the merger possibilities. First, he says, it filled his need for expanding the treaty reinsurance business. "They were a very well-respected name in that field," he says.

In addition, he thought the merger would bring into the organization several people who could run the business. "They would give perpetuity to the company," Stancik says.

Later in 1996, King and the other principals of Morgan, Read and Coleman went to the United States to get a close-up look at the Gallagher organization. They liked what they saw, and the deal closed on September 13, 1996. That Friday the 13th proved to be very lucky for everyone.

"The company has grown beyond our wildest expectations," Stancik says. In 1995, Arthur J. Gallagher (UK) Ltd. did about $20 million in revenues and had about 100 employees. In 2003, it did $78 million in gross revenues and had 320 people. Gallagher (UK) does only wholesale and reinsurance brokerage, and it has expanded into new lines of business, not only in London, but also in Australia, Singapore, the Middle East and Bermuda.

The merger with Morgan, Read and Coleman, Ltd. "kicked Gallagher into being a real Lloyd's broker," Stancik says.

To start the process of being a "real Lloyd's broker," King invited the chairman of Lloyd's to meet with him shortly after the merger. He also did other things to raise the company's profile in the close-knit London insurance world. "We wanted to show we were a permanent presence in the Lloyd's market," he says. "We distinctly wanted to give Gallagher more of a global reach."

Having a major presence in the Lloyd's market is critical for Gallagher's growth as an international broker. Lloyd's occupies a unique place in the insurance world, and no broker can be taken seriously without a connection to Lloyd's. "You need that in your toolbox," Nastri says.

Part of Gallagher's strategy for expansion includes pursuing major corporations, expanding from its traditional base of middle-market clients. The New York office, for example, is aggressively targeting Fortune 500 clients. The London office is especially important as Gallagher goes after these companies.

"We bring Lloyd's and the London market and all its skills to the table for Gallagher retail brokers," King says. Lloyd's is known for its innovation, its ability to place difficult risks and handle challenging situations. These capabilities are critical to landing and serving major clients. "We have no credibility otherwise," King says.

King says the London operation values its relationship with the parent company, and understands the role it plays in the company's success. He notes that Gallagher first needed a London presence to serve the Bishop's Plan for Self-Insurance. "That is still the cornerstone of our business," King says. "We never lose sight of that. It is one big account that has been nonstop in London for 30 to 40 years."

But the majority of the business of Arthur J. Gallagher (UK)–about 80 percent–comes from outside the Gallagher broker network. "We want to be an alternative, not just to Gallagher, but to other brokers as well," King says.

Much of its business also comes from outside North America, and this non-U.S. business will be a significant factor in fueling the expansion of Arthur J. Gallagher & Co., if the company is to continue its exceptional rate of growth. The London operation is essential to attracting and serving this business.

"The London marketplace is arguably the biggest and most vital in the world," says David Ross, chief executive officer of Gallagher (UK) Global Risks Division, a unit of Gallagher (UK). "If we are going to expand outside the U.S., we must have this presence."

King notes that most insurance business from outside the United States and the European Union comes out of those countries as reinsurance. Many non-European and non-U.S. countries require insurance to be written by local insurers, most of which are government-owned or-controlled. That business then is sent out of the country as facultative reinsurance.

In addition, King says, the company does a lot of reinsurance business for Lloyd's syndicates and London companies.

Gallagher (UK) is the fastest-growing broker in London, Ross says, and he expects that to continue. In fact, the impressive growth of the London operation has been one of Gallagher's major successes in the last decade.

"Gallagher London had been a sleeping giant," Nastri says. The expertise and experience of the professionals in London, backed by the reputation of the parent company, have drawn growing numbers of clients. It also has attracted many talented professionals looking for a cultural fit.

A host of London professionals, like their counterparts in the United States, were displaced by the series of mega-mergers that swept through the international insurance world during the 1990s. Many of those professionals, looking for a quality company, brought their considerable skills to Gallagher's London office.

King says that talented people are attracted by a company that is part of the world's fourth-largest broker. But what keeps them, he says, is a sense of working together. He says, "We're not the same as everybody else....We're very good at what we do, but we actually share in each other's ups and downs."

Unlike many of its competitors, Gallagher's London office "has grown for the right reasons," Nastri says. "Ours has been a gradual, structured expansion, for the right reasons—profitability and the culture."

He says that the collegial culture that characterizes the U.S. offices translates easily into London.

"We're not across the road from each other, but there's a family feel about the company," Nastri says. He is especially impressed with the availability and responsiveness of senior management. Like many Gallagher employees, in the U.S. and abroad, he talks about how even the top officers at Gallagher make people feel welcome and appreciated.

For example, he says, he was a friend of John Gallagher, whom he calls "a very inspirational guy." On the day of Nastri's wedding, John sent a telegram of congratulations to the church—a gesture that Nastri has not forgotten. "It sounds a little old-fashioned, but our culture is what makes us different, makes us special," he says.

"Our business is a people business, and our major asset is our people," Nastri says. "If you keep your people happy, it's amazing how the rest of things fall in line."

Chapter 15
The Value Of Independence

"A winner is someone who recognizes his God-given talents, works his tail off to develop them into skills, and uses those skills to accomplish his goals."

Larry Bird

Anyone who has ever piloted a boat, from a dinghy to a battleship, knows that sometimes it is necessary to make a correction to get back on course. In the mid-1990s, Pat Gallagher made just such a correction, reminding recent merger partners of Arthur J. Gallagher & Co. that the benefits brokerage and consulting business is an independent part of the company. • Benefits brokerage and consulting had been an integral part of AJGCo. for decades, growing out of the company's underlying understanding of the value of serving the client. Insurance brokerage is, at its most basic, a relationship business, and being able to provide clients with what they need builds a strong relationship between the client and the broker. It also, of course, adds to the broker's bottom line. • The target market for AJGCo. brokers traditionally has been middle-market companies. By the late 1960s and early 1970s, employee benefits were becoming increasingly important—and expensive—for many of these companies. They needed help in finding providers that could deliver benefits that would keep employees happy without emptying the corporate checking account. Increasingly, they turned to their property/casualty broker for that help. Gallagher was quick to respond to the challenge, and to the opportunity. The company started a benefits business under Warren Van der Voort Sr., who led the effort to sell mass-marketed life, auto and homeowners coverages on a payroll-deduct basis.

The group benefits business was successful, and by the mid-1970s, Gallagher had established a separate Group Department. The Group Department expanded its offerings into self-insured benefits, writing the first self-insured benefits client in 1975; by 1985, AJGCo. had more than 120,000 covered lives. What had begun as a way to provide additional service to P/C clients had evolved into a promising business of its own.

In 1985, Arthur J. Gallagher & Co. was reorganized along product lines. The explosive growth of the company during the 1970s and early 1980s required a more formal corporate structure. As part of this reorganization, Gallagher Benefit Services was created. Bob Gallagher made an important decision in forming Gallagher Benefit Services: He determined that the company's efforts to broker employee benefits had to be kept separate from its property/casualty brokerage business. In most brokerages, placing benefits business was a sort of sideline, with brokers offering benefits as an add-on to other coverages. But Bob knew that for the benefits business to reach its full potential, it needed to be separate and independent.

The decision to build one benefits company within AJGCo. brought with it a need for additional talent to manage the growth. David Ziegler joined Gallagher Benefit Services in 1983 and soon moved to Miami to build the Eastern Region.

Angelo Nardi joined in 1986 and became regional manager of the Central Region.

As merger partners joined Arthur J. Gallagher & Co., however, the line between benefits and P/C brokerage sometimes became blurred. Some merger partners had always run their benefits business as part of their property/casualty brokerage operations, and they were reluctant to reorganize. As a result, two benefits organizations began to evolve–Gallagher Benefit Services, and the benefits business run as part of the P/C sales effort. By the late 1990s, Pat Gallagher decided to make clear what his uncle had proclaimed a decade earlier: The benefits business of Arthur J. Gallagher & Co. would be conducted exclusively by Gallagher Benefit Services.

This separation has been critical to the success of Gallagher Benefit Services, according to Jim Durkin, who has led the division since it was formed in 1985. "We made a decision as a company to create a separate benefits company," Durkin says. Gallagher built a business focused 100 percent on benefits. And Gallagher Benefit Services has grown from $50 million in revenues and 456 employees in 1995 to $159 million in gross revenues and 951 employees in 2003.

Durkin believes that one of the main drivers of the growth of Gallagher Benefit Services has been the ability to recruit top-notch people. And that ability, he says, stems from the decision to create a separate benefits entity. Benefits professionals who work as part of a property/casualty brokerage realize early on that they are second-class citizens, and that their career paths are inevitably blocked. "Sooner or later, you report to the P/C branch manager," Durkin says.

But because Gallagher Benefit Services is a division separate from the P/C brokerage operation, its benefits professionals have unlimited career opportunities. They can participate in growing all aspects of the business. And that, in turn, helps Gallagher Benefit Services grow.

"We have some really strong people who were looking for a chance to be a part of building an organization," Durkin says. "They know that with us, they can go as far as their talent and drive can take them."

Gallagher Benefit Services offers brokerage, consulting and administrative services, helping clients cope with a variety of benefit problems, many of which have worsened in recent years. Health care costs in particular have been rising significantly, while government regulation of benefits has increased. Double-digit cost increases have become the norm, and employers are struggling to provide appropriate care to employees while meeting government guidelines and corporate budgets. Gallagher Benefit Services offers expertise in all the health and welfare benefits, including executive benefits and financial planning, worksite marketing and voluntary products, defined contribution plans, actuarial services, data analysis and benchmarking, retirement services, benefits communication and outsourcing, and human resource services.

The benefits professionals work to meet client needs by taking a comprehensive approach. First, they sit down with a client to develop a strategy, helping the client determine what kinds of benefits to offer and how to structure those benefits.

Once the client decides on a strategy, the Gallagher professionals go into the market to talk to insurers and health maintenance organizations and to put together a program that fulfills that strategy. If a client decides to self-insure, Gallagher Benefit Administrators, a unit of Gallagher Benefit Services, can handle the claims administration.

"We try to figure out what clients need to solve their problems," Durkin says.

Arthur J. Gallagher & Co. has long believed that its clients are best served when talented professionals are allowed to develop and grow. When Art Gallagher's young business began to take off, he hired Dan Wachs and Ed Keating to help him. At first, they handled the back-room part of the business, while Art did the selling. Insurance agencies were commonly set up this way, with the principals doing all the selling, mainly to protect against piracy. If employees did not build relationships with clients, they could not decide to steal those clients and form their own agency.

But Art decided that it was not fair to limit the careers of Wachs and Keating. If they could succeed in sales, he thought, they should be allowed to succeed. It also became clear to Art that letting his employees develop to their full potential only helped his company. After all, the more Wachs and Keating sold, the more money was made by Arthur J. Gallagher & Co.

The decision, first by Bob and then by Pat, to give the benefit professionals the independence they need to succeed continues this Gallagher tradition of believing in its people. "These weren't easy decisions, but they were very important," Durkin says. "This gives people the idea that they are in charge of their own destiny."

The recruiting and retention of extremely qualified and talented people has helped Gallagher Benefit Services expand its capabilities. The division offers special expertise in several industries, and it has established nine niche practice groups: energy, health care, higher education, hospitality, public entity, religious, restaurant, education (K-12) and transportation.

Another spur to the division's growth is the fact that, on an annual basis since about 1995, Gallagher Benefit Services has taken a more formal approach to strategic planning. Durkin meets with management once a year to discuss and evaluate what is going on in their industry, and how they stack up. They develop a plan for Gallagher Benefit Services that includes clear strategic directions and a well-defined plan of action. Then they report back monthly to check on their progress.

"Many of the things we have accomplished have come out of this planning process," Durkin says. For example, they recently established a new business unit called Technical Support and Compliance.

"Our business is inundated with federal and state legislation," Durkin says. Even when that legislation does not directly affect the benefits that Gallagher Benefit Services sells, it can be an enormous burden on clients. The Itasca branch started to centralize regulatory information and other important data about benefits, and to make this information available online to salespeople. This idea grew into the creation of the centralized technical support and compliance team.

Now there are four data bases: health and welfare legislation compliance issues; a resource library, including information on people available to do seminars or provide other information for clients; a document library; and information on professional operating standards. These data bases are available to all Gallagher Benefit Services producers and, Durkin says, "For our sales force, these data bases are their lifelines."

The next step is to make the information available to clients, through their client Web sites. "We're trying to create everything a client needs to manage its benefits and human resources," Durkin says. "That makes it very easy for clients to do business with us, and very hard for them to leave us."

Mergers also have been crucial to the growth of Gallagher Benefit Services, expanding the group's size and breadth and adding expertise in new areas, such as retirement and actuarial consulting and human resources consulting, which includes helping clients develop a strategy for balancing their total spending on salary and benefits. John Caraher, who joined Gallagher Benefit Services in 1993 as vice president of finance, spearheads negotiations with merger partners.

The same qualities that attract talented professionals have helped to attract talented merger partners, Durkin says. "Firms are attracted to us because they see the advantages to being part of this organization," he says.

On the one hand, Gallagher Benefit Services is a separate organization, not a stepchild. Merger partners know they will not be limited by competing interests within the organization. But, at the same time, they understand that they are becoming part of an organization with worldwide name recognition and a fine reputation. Becoming part of Gallagher will greatly enhance their capabilities and reach.

Durkin sees mergers as an ongoing avenue to growth, and Gallagher Benefit Services has recently hired a person to prospect full-time for merger partners. "We've dramatically stepped up our merger activity, and we'll continue to step it up," Durkin says.

Jim Durkin has been with Gallagher since 1976. He believes that the qualities that have brought success to Gallagher Benefit Services are rooted firmly in the company's history and culture. Chief among these is a strong commitment to serving the client, and to being able to bring all the resources necessary to bear on solving a client's problem. As the cost and importance of employee benefits has grown, so has the client's need for help in designing and placing benefit plans.

And, Durkin says, the other major factor in the division's success—the commitment to letting people reach their full potential—also is central to the culture of the parent company.

"This company's culture gives people the opportunity to succeed," he says. "The formula is simple: Give people the opportunity to succeed, help them when they don't get it right, and when they get it right, cheer like hell."

Chapter 16
Finding A Niche

"Everyone lives by selling something."

Robert Louis Stevenson

The Brokerage Services Retail Division (BSD Retail) of Arthur J. Gallagher & Co., under the direction of Jim Gault, brokers all types of property/casualty insurance, and it serves clients in a wide variety of industries. More than half its business, though, is conducted through some 20 niche practices–cross-divisional groups that offer exceptional expertise and a large client base in a specific area. This niche strategy focuses on the development of products and services specific to each niche industry, and it aids in the attraction and retention of clients in those industries. It will become increasingly important to BSD Retail, as the division continues to respond to customers' demands for greater understanding of their businesses. • The niche strategy was embraced officially by BSD Retail at the end of the 20th century, but it had long been an integral part of the company's approach to serving clients. The philosophy behind niches–the idea that the customer is best served when the broker understands the nuances of the customer's business–has always been central to the Gallagher philosophy.

In fact, the company first achieved national exposure when it developed a unique approach to coverage in what was to become a niche dominated by Gallagher. The Bishop's Plan for Self-Insurance was designed after the Archdiocese of Chicago found itself woefully underinsured in the wake of a tragic fire at Our Lady of the Angels Catholic School on December 1, 1958. Ninety-five people, almost all of them elementary school children, died in the fire, and many others were injured. All claims from the fire eventually were adjudicated, and losses were in the multimillions. But the archdiocese had only $100,000 in liability coverage on Our Lady of the Angels Parish.

Bishop Cletus O'Donnell, who was an official in the archdiocese's chancery office at the time, asked his friends the Gallaghers if they could help the church improve its protection of its flock. Bob and John Gallagher, Dan Wachs and Ed Keating suggested a revolutionary idea that replaced the crazy-quilt approach to coverage, much of it purchased at the parish level, with a plan that brought together all the archdiocese's insurance needs. The all-lines protected self-insurance plan that they devised provided 10 times the coverage at half the cost. After the Archdiocese of Chicago signed on, the Gallaghers took the Bishop's Plan on the road, eventually becoming a leading broker for religious entities.

That plan was adapted to the needs of schools and public entities–two other niches in which AJGCo. has become an important player. As those early niches developed, it became obvious to the Gallagher sales force that hands-on, intimate knowledge of the client's business helped them land accounts and was essential in developing the best possible coverage strategy for clients.

By the late 1990s, clients knew it too. Increasingly, clients expected their brokers to have a grasp of the specifics of their businesses. "Over the mid to late '90s, we had come to the understanding that people had to be specialists," says Jim Braniff, former head of BSD Retail and now manager of the South Central Region. "That's what buyers were expecting."

Tom Gallagher, who is now president of Arthur J. Gallagher & Co. Risk Management Services Inc., saw the power of specialization firsthand. On June 30, 1996, AJGCo. acquired Lamberson, Koster and Co. in San Francisco, the preeminent construction broker west of the Mississippi River and one of the top construction brokers in the country. A few months later, Tom Gallagher went to San Francisco to take over as president of the newly acquired agency. "I saw something that was absolutely amazing," he says. "They saw themselves as being in the construction business rather than in the insurance business."

Gallagher believed that Lamberson, Koster and Co. was "an extraordinary example of how, when you have a niche focus, you can do the business really well." And, he says, "I thought, 'This is something we can do all over the place.'" Tom Gallagher went on to develop the construction niche for AJGCo., and the niche had grown to $54 million in gross revenues in 2003. It is still headquartered in San Francisco, with practice groups in Houston, Boston, New York, Chicago, Milwaukee, Dallas and Seattle.

Although the niche idea had long been employed by Gallagher brokers, conversations about making it an official part of the company's organizational structure began in the fall of 1998. At that time, Gary Van der Voort was named national niche director to coordinate the effort.

In late 1998, BSD Retail management started the process by gathering information about the number of clients and the amount of revenues the company already had in various business areas. They determined levels of revenues and clients necessary to establish a niche, and those business areas that met or exceeded these levels became the first niches.

BSD Retail now recognizes some 20 niches in which the company has exceptional expertise. Those niches have helped to drive growth for BSD Retail, which had gross revenues of $564 million in 2003, up from $259 million in 1998, when the strategy was implemented. That in turn drives growth for Arthur J. Gallagher & Co., because BSD Retail accounts for 42 percent of the revenues of the company.

Jim Braniff, who took over from Van der Voort as head of BSD Retail, says buyers drove the niche strategy. "Buyers were looking for expertise by industry, and in order to deliver that, we had to aggregate our expertise," he says.

Van der Voort adds, "In today's environment, your knowledge of insurance is assumed by most buyers. They are looking for brokers who are very experienced in the client's business."

The niche strategy allows Gallagher to leverage its position with the markets, as well as to combine forces in areas such as education. "You need education," Braniff says. "You have to keep getting better and better. One of the main values of the niche approach is that it continues to develop expertise.

"This is both a knowledge and a relationship business," he says. "Even if you have the relationships, if you don't have the knowledge, you're toast."

Gallagher has made a full commitment to developing this knowledge and to making it available throughout the company, Braniff says. And Gallagher producers are expected to use the knowledge developed by the niches to prepare themselves for sales calls. "We have told our people that we are not willing to put our resources behind a producer going after an account if he does not have the right expertise," Braniff says.

Niche practice groups also enable the company to consolidate and focus efforts in areas such as promotion, advertising, and developing value-added programs and services that provide special advantages for clients and potential clients within the niches.

The process begins with identifying a niche–an area in which Gallagher already is doing significant business or on which the company intends to concentrate. Once a niche is identified, a niche manager is named. The niche manager is responsible for coordinating communication and information within the niche, and between the niche and the rest of the company. Sam Babington is manager of the Mergers and Acquisitions Niche. Professionals in this niche work with companies that are involved in acquisitions to ensure that they have the proper insurance coverage. For example, if due diligence uncovers a problem, they might need an insurance product to protect them against fallout from that problem. Gallagher also brokers traditional P/C coverages for companies involved in these deals.

Babington believes that one of the hallmarks of the Gallagher niche strategy–and one of the things that sets it apart from other companies–is that Gallagher brokers understand both the client and the market. This stems from the company's earliest days, when Art Gallagher decided against having separate "back room" people and salespeople. Instead, he wanted all his company's salespeople to understand both the sales and the technical aspects of the business. This expanded understanding encourages exceptional creativity, and, Babington says,

"When you get creative people teaming up, you're going to get explosive growth."

Part of the responsibility of the niche manager is to ensure that expertise in a niche is coordinated and made available to all Gallagher salespeople. If someone is visiting a client in the hospitality industry, for example, the salesperson can call on all the resources of the hospitality niche to help make the sale and service the account.

Alexandria Glickman, who runs the Real Estate and Hospitality Niche, works with the markets to develop product, and she also is available to work with anyone in the Gallagher organization who needs her help. She says, "I feel like the point guard on a basketball team."

Steven Ring is the managing director of the Public Entity and Scholastic Niche, one of the company's biggest niches, with about $65 million in revenues. As the niche director, he says, his job is to "provide the resources, support and product for our salespeople to sell." He and his team help manage market relationships, provide support and work to solve problems and deal with issues. They also foster teamwork, holding an annual meeting for all producers as well as other meetings throughout the year. The managing directors try to establish "a culture within a culture," he says. They promote the mantra, "Put our best resources forward to give us the best chance of getting the account."

Dave Marcus, who also works with the Public Entity and Scholastic Niche, believes that the Gallagher emphasis on teamwork makes the niche strategy even more effective. "We are team players, and that comes from the top down and the bottom up," he says.

The Public Entity and Scholastic Niche is one of the company's most successful niches, but Marcus is not content. "We want to be the best public sector and scholastic broker out there," he says. "Our focus on specialization is one of the main reasons we have grown. It is all about people and about making yourself very, very good in your area of expertise."

Tom Gallagher says that "the niches all have their own personality." But, he says, they are united in their commitment to helping the company attract and serve clients. "The whole niche strategy is about serving customers," he says. "There are no territorial issues."

Jim McFarlane, chairman of BSD Retail's West Coast Region, calls the niche strategy "one of the best things we've ever done. People today want to deal with people who have intellectual capital," and the strategy allows Gallagher to develop that capital. Clients have come to believe that the expertise Gallagher has developed in its various niches can be counted on to provide them with the best answers to their questions.

"I tell people, 'If I say it's going to rain, bring an umbrella. If I say it's Easter, you can paint your eggs, because it's going to happen,'" he says. And clients have come to rely on that.

Some of the Gallagher niches, such as religious and public entities, have been around for decades. But the company is always looking for new opportunities to apply its strategy to develop new areas of business. Phil Norton, who is president of BSD Retail's Professional Liability Division and managing director of the E&O and D&O Niche, joined the company on December 31, 1998. He was hired to develop a niche in professional liability, focusing on errors and omissions and directors and officers coverages. Developing expertise in these areas had become critical to Gallagher's efforts to secure large accounts, he says.

The knowledge and resources provided through the D&O and E&O Niche have made Arthur J. Gallagher & Co. much better able to compete for major accounts, bringing on board several Fortune 1000 companies. The niche has grown tenfold in about five years.

"You are not saying to the client, 'I can do everything,' because clients don't believe that," Norton says. "Instead, you're saying, 'I understand this business. I've done my homework, I've organized my resources, and that allows me to provide more to the client.'" That is a message that clients can embrace.

Gallagher Gallery II

CEO Pat Gallagher (left) and Chairman Bob Gallagher have piloted the company founded as a one-man shop by their grandfather and father into one of the top insurance brokerages in the world.

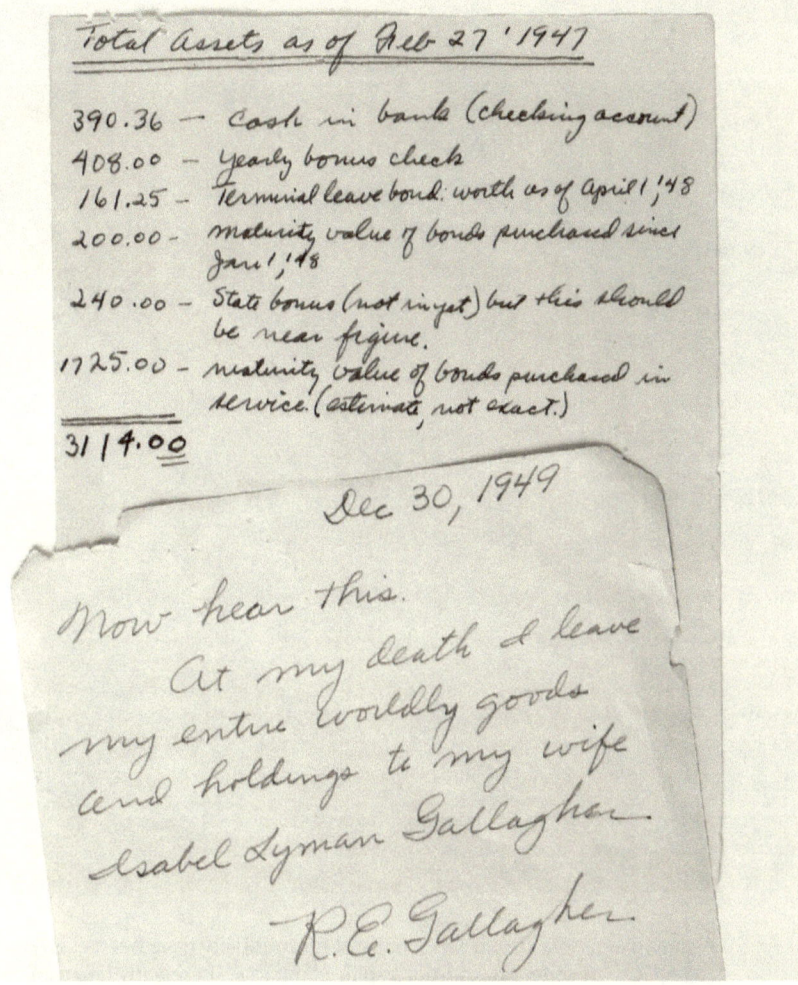

Total assets as of Feb 27 '1947

390.36 — Cash in bank (checking account)
408.00 — Yearly bonus check
161.25 — Terminal leave bond. worth as of April 1, '48
200.00 — maturity value of bonds purchased since Jan 1, '48
240.00 — State bonus (not in yet) but this should be near figure.
1725.00 — maturity value of bonds purchased in service. (estimate, not exact.)
3114.00

Dec 30, 1949

Now hear this.
At my death I leave my entire worldly goods and holdings to my wife Isabel Lyman Gallagher.

R. E. Gallagher

The success of AJGCo. is due largely to the hard work and sacrifice of its many employees. Among the early employees was a young salesman named Bob Gallagher, who outlined his assets in detail in 1947. In 1949, Bob was recently married and prepared to leave all of those assets to his wife, Isabel.

BUDGET FOR YR. '48

130.70 TAKE HOME BASE
 50.00 FLIGHT PAY
180.70

FIXED COSTS PER MONTH

INVESTMENTS: 37.50
INSURANCE: 6.50
BANK SAFE CHARGE: .50
                    44.50

ADDED COSTS PER MONTH

1. MEALS   1.20 / DAY (AV. MONTH 25 DAYS) - - -   30.00
2. CLOTHES - -   -   -   -   -   -   -   - -   15.00
3. TRANSPORTATION. -   -   -   -   -   -   - - -   10.00
4. ENTERTAINMENT - 15./WEEK   -   -   - - - -   60.00
5. SLUSH FUND FOR -   -   -   -   -   -   - - -   21.20
        a. INCIDENTALS
        B. CHRISTMAS
        c. ADDED SAVING FOR STOCKS
        D. RING OR CAR
        E. PRESENTS

ANY MONTHLY SAVINGS IN 1,2,3,4, GO INTO 5.
BUILD UP AND KEEP RESERVE OF 100.00 IN 5,
ALL ABOVE THIS INVEST.

A clear plan and a strong sense of fiscal responsibility have been central to AJGCo.'s rise to a billion-dollar-plus company. These early financial notes from Chairman Bob Gallagher are evidence that these attributes existed when there was considerably less than $1 billion at stake.

This cover of the company magazine, The Confidential, celebrated
Arthur J. Gallagher & Co. reaching the $1 billion mark.

A mere 75 years after its founding, Arthur J. Gallagher & Co. had become one of the top insurance brokerage companies in the world.

A strong summer intern program has been a part of AJGCo. for decades, and many of the company's top executives, including CEO Pat Gallagher, are alumni of the program. This group, the first-year 2004 interns, may hold future Gallagher leaders.

The Gallagher Scholars are a personal philanthropic effort of Chairman Bob Gallagher and his wife, Isabel (center). The Gallaghers offer scholarships to deserving students at Catholic schools in Chicago's inner city.

The Executive Management Committee, made up of AJGCo.'s operating managers, acts as an important advisory committee to the Board of Directors. Members of the Executive Management Committee are (back, from left) John Rosengren, Jim Durkin and Jim Gault, and (front, from left) Dave McGurn, Rich McKenna and Doug Howell.

Arthur J. Gallagher & Co. was one of the first companies in the industry
to remove virtually all insiders from its Board of Directors. The company's board includes (back, from left) Elbert Hand, T. Kimball Brooker,
Bob Gallagher, David Johnson, and (front, from left) Bernard Henges-
baugh, James Wimmer, Pat Gallagher, Gary Coughlan and Ilene Gordon.

Top: New CFO Doug Howell (left) and Sally Wasikowski are among those who provide financial leadership to AJGCo. Bottom: Wally Bryce (left) and Bob Gallagher Jr. help develop the company's technical expertise.

Gallagher Bassett executives include (top, from left) Norm Darling and Emil Bravo, and (bottom, from left) Russell Parsons and Peter Searson.

Among the leaders of Gallagher Benefit Services are (top, from left)
David Ziegler and Angelo Nardi, and (bottom) John Caraher.

Critical to the niche strategy of Brokerage Services Retail are (top, from left) Sam Babington and Tom Gallagher, and (bottom from left) Phil Norton and Dave Marcus.

Among the developers of Brokerage Services Retail's niche strategy are (top, from left) Jim McFarlane and Steven Ring, and (bottom, from left) Craig Van der Voort and Jim Braniff.

Mega-mergers at other brokers brought exceptional new talent to AJGCo., including Alexandria Glickman (bottom). The new Brokerage Services Retail office in New York, home to (top, from left) Doug Brown and John McCaffrey, benefits especially from the experience of these additions to the Gallagher family.

The U.S. presence of the Specialty Marketing and International Division includes (top, from left) Joel Cavaness and Jeff McNatt, and (bottom, from left) Joe Nelligan and Randy Jensen.

Part of the team at the Specialty Marketing and International Division
are (top, from left) Jay Woods in the U.S. and Steve Prince, and (bottom,
from left) Philip Nastri and Brian King in the U.K.

The Specialty Marketing and International Division handles most of AJGCo.'s overseas operations. David Ross (top left) is central to those efforts in the United Kingdom, and Jennifer Gallagher and David McManus work through the Bermuda office.

Chapter 17
A Nation Of Immigrants

"Do not be afraid to take a big step. You can't cross a chasm in two small jumps."

David Lloyd George

Brokerage Services Retail is the largest division of Arthur J. Gallagher & Co., so decisions to make changes in the organization of that division are not taken lightly. But at the dawn of the 21st century, the company made several moves that positioned it to benefit from events in the market. • In 1998, the division began working with a professional planner to write a long-range plan for growth. As a result of that plan, says Jim Gault, who heads the Brokerage Services Retail Division, "We have transformed Brokerage Services." • The planner realized that Arthur J. Gallagher & Co. had grown into a major player in the insurance brokerage market. It was handling larger and larger clients, and it increasingly was being seen by clients as one of the top firms in the world. • The company had accomplished this growth, since the beginning, through timely and careful selection of merger partners and through organic growth within the existing organization. The planners knew that this strategy for growth would continue to be successful. They also realized that the company was in a unique position to boost its organic growth by tapping into some of the top talent in the industry.

The planners saw that their industry was in a period of chaos. Merger mania at the very top of the brokerage world was resulting in large, long-standing companies being absorbed into other large, long-standing companies. Although Arthur J. Gallagher & Co. decided not to participate in the merger activity at the top, it moved quickly to benefit from the fallout.

"Merger mania was great for us," Gault says, because it created a unique opportunity to bring on board some exceptional producers. Gallagher was becoming recognized as an up-and-coming company, a company with a very bright future that could offer good people a chance to do very well. At the same time, there were many people whose jobs had been disrupted by the mergers. They found themselves working for new companies, with new bosses and new cultures. Some of these people were not comfortable with their new situations, and they were looking for other options.

Gallagher provided an option, says Gary Van der Voort, the company's national niche director. "Our biggest competitors made it easy for us to attract some of their best people," he says.

Jim Braniff, now manager of the South Central Region, headed BSD Retail at the time. "I talked to hundreds of producers," Braniff says. "They were not happy with the culture where they were, so they came to us." What they discovered at Gallagher was a culture that stressed teamwork, integrity and hard work. They found a culture that believed in its people and gave them the support they needed to succeed. "We tell people, this culture is real, and we expect you to live it," Braniff says.

Many of the producers he talked to decided they wanted to live the Gallagher culture. In all, the division hired 140 new producers during an 18-month period from 2001 to the middle of 2002. "That was huge," Gault says. "We hadn't hired 100 new producers in the whole decade of the '90s."

Alexandria Glickman was one of those new hires, coming to Gallagher from Marsh & McLennan and Johnson & Higgins. She is now area executive vice president in Los Angeles and head of the Real Estate and Hospitality Niche. She is one of Gallagher's leading producers and the #1 real estate broker in the United States.

She was a very successful producer in her previous job, but she was uncomfortable in the culture. She wanted something more, and she was not alone. She says, "Gallagher in the last five years is a nation of immigrants." Like travelers coming to a new homeland, producers have journeyed to Gallagher from competing brokers, looking for a place where they can set down roots.

Glickman came to Gallagher, she says, because "it was a new opportunity, and because of the culture. The culture is a wonderful combination of very aggressive and very hometown Midwestern." It is hard-driving and results-oriented without being arrogant and heartless. And she is happy that she made the move, for her sake and for the sake of her clients.

"Here the client is well-served. I feel like a trustee of the client. Gallagher gives me the opportunity to do that," she says. "I like going to work in the morning."

There were some in the industry who thought that Gallagher's producer expansion was a mistake. Many of the new hires had non-compete agreements with their former employers that limited their sales efforts, at least temporarily. In addition, the market was coming off a difficult period, and many companies were keeping their head down and trying to survive. Some analysts thought that Gallagher was taking too big a chance, spending an awful lot of money for a questionable return.

Even though the market had begun to harden and business was improving for the industry overall, some analysts were still skeptical. "They thought we were blowing the uptick of a hard market," Pat Gallagher says. But the company was confident of its strategy and stood by its decision. "One of the things about us is that we are playing for the long term," Pat says. "We work our way through problems."

Van der Voort notes that the decision to make the hires was consistent with the company's approach to doing business. "We invested in the future," he says. "Our assets are our people, and it was a great opportunity to bring on some good people."

Not all analysts were skeptical. In Business Insurance's 2003 agent/broker profile issue, Hugh Warns, a vice president and equities research analyst with J. P. Morgan Chase & Co. in Baltimore, supports the move. He estimates that Gallagher spent about $15 million to bring on board producers who have the potential to generate between $60 million and $80 million of business annually within the next few years. The strategy "makes a lot of sense," he says.

That opinion likely will be shared by more and more observers as the results show up on the bottom line. Gallagher's remarkable investment in talent already has started to pay off all around the company—but perhaps nowhere as dramatically as in New York City.

When Doug Brown, area president in New York, joined Gallagher in April 2002, the brokerage division shared an office at 14 Wall Street with AJGCo. reinsurance and benefits operations. Brokerage Services Retail had six people in that office, servicing one account. It was a situation that could not be allowed to continue.

"The company was becoming a $1 billion organization with no significant representation in New York," Brown says. If Gallagher was serious about becoming a world-class brokerage firm and going after large accounts, it needed a much greater presence in New York, where many of those accounts were headquartered.

Gallagher was serious, and the company decided to open a New York brokerage office. In an exceptionally bold move, management decided to open the office immediately, before there was additional business to support it. They knew they could not get that business until they had the kind of office that would make potential clients take notice. They decided to start from scratch.

"To do a scratch startup in New York is pretty much unheard-of," Brown says. It is extremely expensive, and the payoff might be awhile in coming. "New York has a lot of big-name accounts, but they don't always move very quickly," Brown says.

"That was a very bold decision for Gallagher to make," John McCaffrey says. "From Gallagher's point of view, it was a real leap of faith. Kind of like, Build it, and they will come....A lot of companies will not make that kind of investment. It shows the confidence the Gallagher people have in their name and their company."

Brimming with that confidence, Gallagher decided to rent one floor—about 10,000 square feet—at 444 Madison Avenue, and they moved in in June 2002. Staffing was more challenging.

"We built the office across the board," Brown says. "You start with people." He identified people with a strong expertise and reputation in property/casualty and liability coverages, and he brought several of them into the new office. The company also hired support people, again looking for the best in the business.

Many of the people Brown hired came because they were looking for a chance to make a difference. They were intrigued and excited about the opportunity to get involved from the start, and they relished the chance to be able to put their mark on the bold experiment that Gallagher was conducting in Manhattan.

People also came because they were intrigued by the Gallagher culture, Brown says. "The culture here is intact and entrepreneurial," he says. "It is very externally focused on the client."

When the office held its grand opening in September 2002, there were fewer than 10 producers and about 20 to 25 people in all. But they were clearly poised for growth.

And grow they did. In the first year, 2002, the office did $2.5 million in revenues. But in its second year, it did $10 million in revenues. New people joined, too, and by the end of 2003, there were 12 producers and about 50 total employees. People were sharing office space and phones, and the company decided to take another floor in the building.

The office has accomplished the goal of ensuring Arthur J. Gallagher & Co. a permanent spot on the New York landscape. Professionals in the office now service several Fortune 1000 accounts, as well as the more traditional middle-market accounts. They also offer a private client group, which provides personal lines coverages for wealthy clients. And they refer considerable business to Gallagher's London and Bermuda operations.

McCaffrey believes few companies could have accomplished what Arthur J. Gallagher & Co. did in New York. It was Gallagher's unique approach that helped make the success possible.

"This is a very inclusive organization," he says. "No one at Gallagher thinks he has all the right answers." Instead, the top people at Gallagher listen—to their people, to their clients and to their markets. In New York, McCaffrey says, "They listened to the people who were responsible for the results, and they supported those people....They have confidence in the abilities of the people they give assignments to."

The New York effort also relies heavily on the cultural value of teamwork. "Everybody has brought something to the table," Brown says. "People work very well together here. It's a strong team."

And, he adds, "It's a lot of fun."

At Arthur J. Gallagher & Co., Brown says, working hard to accomplish a common goal is what the company is all about. The people who came together in New York work very hard, knowing that their work is seen and appreciated by their company.

They are coming to understand what the "old-timers" have known for a long time. Pete Durkalski, vice president of operations support for the Brokerage Services Retail Division, joined AJGCo. full-time in 1973. He says, "What has pulled us out of the hard times is our culture, and it is unique in the industry."

Chapter 18
Gallagher Bassett

"Experience is not what happens to you; it is what you do with what happens to you."

Aldous Huxley

An airliner was silhouetted against the September morning sky. Not an unusual sight over New York City. But then something went terribly wrong, as the plane banked and headed directly for the World Trade Center. By the time the nightmare was over, about 3,000 people were dead at the hands of terrorists using airplanes as bombs. The attacks of September 11, 2001, were the first on American soil since Pearl Harbor, and the most devastating. • The country, and the world, reeled in the wake of those attacks. The nation grieved, and the world grieved with it. Gradually, however, grief was joined by a determination to carry on, not to fall victim to the ultimate terrorist threat: fear. • Still, life was changed. In some ways, it was changed forever. A kind of innocence was lost as a horrified people watched the towers burn and crumble, saw the Pentagon hit and heard stories of heroism in those buildings and in the skies over Pennsylvania. That innocence may never be fully recovered. • Business, too, was devastated by the events of September 11 and the days that followed. The New York Stock Exchange finally reopened on September 17, and in that first week it fell 11.2 percent.

The insurance world was especially hard-hit. Several of Gallagher's competitors, especially Marsh & McLennan and Aon, lost hundreds of employees in the attacks, and Gallagher set aside competition to join in the grieving.

For a long time, people seemed to want to stick close to home. Certain industries, such as airlines, hotels and restaurants, saw sales plummet. The businesses that serve those companies also began to feel the effects.

Gallagher Bassett Services (GB) is one of those businesses. GB is the major risk management division of Arthur J. Gallagher & Co., and much of its business comes from handling property/casualty claims for clients. About half its clients are in industries that were hit hard by September 11, GB President Rich McKenna says. And when business faltered for these clients, GB suffered as well. In August 2001, GB handled 40,000 claims. But in December 2001, the company handled only 27,000.

Some companies might have panicked, pulling back and laying off people. But Gallagher Bassett's managers believed that what they were experiencing was only a temporary setback. They believed in the ability of their country to weather the crisis, and they believed in the division's ability to prevail as well.

"We look at that period as an example of Gallagher Bassett's commitment to maintaining its workforce," McKenna says. To cut back would be to leave the division unprepared for the recovery it was certain would come.

That faith was well-placed. By the end of 2002, claims levels had surpassed the pre-September 11 levels, and Gallagher Bassett had become the largest multiline third-party claims administrator (TPA) in the world. In 2003, GB posted a very healthy 15 percent organic revenue growth.

Gallagher Bassett has been a substantial contributor to Arthur J. Gallagher & Co. since GB's creation on November 10, 1962. GB was formed by the Gallaghers and Sterling Bassett expressly to serve the needs of AJGCo.'s largest client, Beatrice Foods, as Beatrice implemented a then-revolutionary self-insurance program.

As time passed, GB was called upon to serve other Gallagher clients, including the Bishop's Plan for Self-Insurance. It soon became clear that Gallagher Bassett was among the top claims-handling and risk management entities in the country, and Gallagher brokers had a powerful tool in their sales arsenal.

In the early 1980s, there was a spasm in the insurance market. Liability coverages were vastly curtailed and rates were raised to astronomic heights. As a result, the alternative market became much more attractive to companies—and the need for GB became much greater. It was growing increasingly obvious that there could be a lot of business available to Gallagher Bassett from outside the Gallagher brokerage network.

Bob Gallagher decided to let Gallagher Bassett sell its services independently. It was a very unpopular decision at the time, because the Gallagher brokers felt they owned Gallagher Bassett. But Bob stuck to his guns, and by 1988, Gallagher Bassett had become a completely separate entity.

"That was a seminal moment," Pat says. "Gallagher Basset is clearly independent in the way they're viewed in the marketplace, and that's a fantastic thing." It has been the most important factor in Gallagher Bassett's strong growth, from about $38 million in gross revenues in 1988 to about $293 million in gross revenues in 2003. About 80 percent of GB's business comes from non-Gallagher brokers.

Although GB does 90 percent of its business in the United States, it has 120 offices around the world. One of its recent international success stories has been the development of its franchise in Australia. In 1997, Gallagher Bassett acquired a 50 percent interest in an Australian loss-adjusting firm called Wyatt. In 2003, GB bought out its partner and became full owner of Wyatt Gallagher Bassett, under the direction of Chairman Peter Searson. Wyatt Gallagher Bassett is one of the largest third-party administrators in Australia.

"Wyatt Gallagher Bassett complements the growth of risk management on a worldwide basis," McKenna says. "It allows us to 'plant the flag' on a new continent, and it keeps us on the cutting edge of risk management practices."

Bob Gallagher is fond of saying that, "60 percent of every insurance dollar, ruble or rupee in the world is claims." And Gallagher Bassett has become the preeminent company at capturing those dollars, rubles and rupees. It provides claims management services for a wide range of programs, including workers compensation, liability, auto and property. In addition, it offers information services, loss control consulting and appraisal services.

Much of Gallagher Bassett's success is due to what McKenna calls its "extraordinarily high" retention of business. Well over 90 percent of clients remain with Gallagher Bassett. As a result, when the company adds new business, "we are building on a very solid base," McKenna says.

GB keeps its customers because it can consistently provide what they need. "We deliver the product," says Emil Bravo, executive vice president of Gallagher Bassett. "We service what we sell. We don't overpromise."

Norm Darling, executive vice president and chief operations officer, adds that Gallagher Basset has developed "a strong reputation as being the low-cost provider."

Darling says that when he talks to analysts, he tells them the division's strength comes from several areas. First, there is a stable, experienced senior management team with long tenure both in the industry and at Gallagher Bassett. GB has a long history of promoting from within, and most of its management started out with a background in claims adjustment. As a result, Darling says, they know all aspects of the business, and they respond very quickly to customer issues. "We're very customer-focused," he says. Even top management is ready and able to do whatever is needed to keep the customer satisfied. "We have an open-door policy, both internally and externally, and that is unusual in our industry," Darling says.

In addition, GB aggressively recruits to find talented new professionals. While competitors often lay off people when business gets slow, Gallagher Bassett maintains a strong staff in all markets. The company, as evidenced in the wake of September 11, is committed to the future. Customers appreciate this commitment, Darling says, adding, "They know we are not a short-term player."

Gallagher Bassett also is committed to quality in its products and services, and to creating a quality work environment for its employees. GB was an early leader in the quality improvement movement of the early 1990s. In about 1991, Pete Durkalski, then head of GB, and others investigated the various approaches to quality control. "We already had many of the fundamentals, but we wanted to take it to the next level," Durkalski says. Eventually, they hired quality guru Phil Crosby to help design and launch a program specific to Gallagher Bassett. "The idea was to come up with a common language and a common methodology" that would identify how quality could be improved and how the company could operate more efficiently, Durkalski says.

Once the program was established, Durkalski says, "we integrated it into the whole GB culture." All the functionalities within GB worked together to ensure the highest possible quality. That obviously benefits the client, and it also benefits GB, because it is more cost-efficient when work is done right the first time.

"To this day, every new Gallagher Bassett employee goes through quality training," Durkalski says. "We see the training as neither a beginning nor an end, but a journey. It's about continuous improvement."

Perhaps the biggest plus that GB brings to the table, though, is an exceptional technical capability that helps it keep costs low while delivering unparalleled customer service. The centerpiece of Gallagher Bassett is Risx-Facs, its electronic claims and loss control information management system.

When Risx-Facs was introduced in 1983, it revolutionized the claims administration industry. Because it was an online, real-time information system with enormous capacity, it gave GB the ability to provide accurate, complete information immediately. And information is the life blood of claims management.

"Our clients trust us to spend more than $3 billion of their claims money each year," McKenna says. "We need to be able to show where every penny of that money goes." Risx-Facs is the mechanism for showing where the money goes. Clients tap into the risxfacs.com data base 12 million times a month, McKenna says. By the end of 2003, the system had more than 7,500 users.

Risx-Facs is differentiated from other claims management systems by its expandability, flexibility and accuracy, Darling says. The system is virtually infinitely expandable, with little or no disruption to the client. It is designed to be modular, so that new modules can be added as a client's desire for data increases. There is no need to inconvenience the client by shutting the system down or installing new hardware or software.

At the same time, it is flexible enough to meet client demands easily and quickly. For example, a major client was involved in a merger situation and needed data. Using Risx-Facs, Gallagher Bassett was able to find the data and get it into the client's hands within an hour or two. The potential merger partner, which did not use Gallagher Bassett services, took days to locate its data.

Flexibility and expandability would mean nothing, though, if the data were not accurate. Gallagher Bassett's Risx-Facs has a reputation as being the most accurate information system in the industry.

Gallagher Bassett is committed to continually improving its standard-setting technical capabilities, with the goal of making business smoother for clients as well as GB. To that end, Gallagher Bassett is hoping to achieve a paperless or nearly paperless operation, in which reports would be sent electronically, making them instantly accessible to clients and claims people alike. Currently, about 80 percent of reports are sent electronically.

Gallagher Bassett expects to continue to grow, especially in the areas of major corporate accounts, captives and outsourcing of insurance company claims departments. The division is confident that it will be able to maintain its extremely high business retention rate while developing significant additional new business.

The reason for this confidence is simple. Darling says, "Client satisfaction is what it's all about. Your reputation grows, and that's a big reason clients come to you."

Chapter 19
Investing In The Future

"Experience is a hard teacher because she gives the test first, the lesson afterward."

Vernon Law

Doug Howell joined Arthur J. Gallagher & Co. as chief financial officer in March 2003. The company had been without a CFO for about six months, so Howell had to hit the ground running. Howell was hired because he had the kind of operational expertise that would be required to support the growth that AJGCo. had been experiencing and expected to continue to experience. He was the man to paint the company's financial picture in the new century. • Among the decisions that Howell made shortly after he was hired was to scale back considerably on Gallagher's outside investing. "We want to get back to doing what we know best," he says. "We want to use the company's profits to invest in the company." • During the latter part of 2002 and the first quarter of 2003, Gallagher wrote off $70 million in investments. Virtually all of these were venture capital investments, many of them in dot.com companies that had suffered in the bursting of the technology bubble. The company retains several other investments, many of which it has had for decades and which are very profitable. But going forward, Howell says, the plan is to reinvest the company's cash in the company, by acquiring merger partners, raising dividends and buying back company stock.

Most of Gallagher's investment decisions are implemented by AJG Financial Services, which was formed in 1996 as an outgrowth of the company's investment activities. Those activities were growing, and the company wanted to formally recognize the financial services team as a profit center.

At the time, the company's investments were mainly tax-oriented, in areas like alternative fuels and low-income housing. When AJG Financial Services was formed, the investments were expanded. For example, says Mark Strauch, executive vice president of AJG Financial Services, the focus moved from investing in low-income housing to investing in the companies that develop low-income housing. "The difference is becoming an active versus a passive investor," Strauch says.

The company has been a longtime investor in alternative fuels and energy sources. Gallagher started on this course in 1990, investing in landfill gas projects. These projects use gas created in landfills to run generators, which in turn create electricity. Gallagher has investments in several landfill gas projects, and each one generates tax credits and/or operational profits.

In 1996, Gallagher began investing in synthetic coal. The company eventually developed four synthetic coal projects, and each one can generate substantial tax credits each year. In all, the waste-to-energy, low-income housing and synthetic coal investments have helped reduce Gallagher's tax rate considerably–to 11.7

percent in 2001, 30 percent in 2002 and 24 percent in 2003. That, of course, is good news for the company's bottom line–and for its investors.

It is also good news for the country. In addition to creating tax credits for Gallagher, these efforts are helping to reduce American dependence on foreign oil–a critical concern in this time of turmoil and unrest in the Middle East, which is the source of much of the world's oil.

"We are experts in energy investing," Howell says. "It is the right thing to do for America, and the right thing to do for our company's investors."

The company also has a successful investment in Asset Alliance Corp., a New York-based company that has ownership in hedge fund managers. Gallagher has a 25 percent minority interest in Asset Alliance, which generally has a 50 percent ownership in 13 fund manager companies with $4 billion under management.

"Just like Gallagher buys insurance agencies, Asset Alliance buys money managers," says Dave Long, president of AJG Financial Services. Gallagher was the lead investor when Asset Alliance was formed in 1996, and Asset Alliance has "done very well," Strauch says.

Gallagher also has real estate investments, including its 60 percent ownership of the 25-story office building in Itasca, Illinois, that serves as the home office. AJGCo. currently occupies about 60 percent of the building.

And AJGCo. owns 80 percent of a partnership that is developing Harmony, Florida, a planned residential community on 11,000 acres near Orlando. The focal point of the development will be a Johnny Miller Signature golf course, which has been designed to showcase and preserve the natural environment of the area.

A high school is set to open in Harmony in 2004, and an elementary school, called the Arthur J. Gallagher Neighborhood School, already is open. More than 60 homes are built or under construction, and when the development is complete, it will have up to 7,200 residential units, as well as commercial retail and light industrial development.

AJG Financial Services is aided in many of its investment interests by the reputation of its parent company. "When we go out to talk to partners and companies about doing a deal, there is a tremendous benefit to having a high-integrity culture," says Sally Wasikowski, vice president of AJG Financial Services.

The investment strategy pursued by AJG Financial Services is designed to help strengthen the company's financial position by reducing its taxes and strengthening its balance sheet. It provides a sort of cushion to help protect the company against the inevitable bumps in the road.

Bob Gallagher says he is proud of the investments the company has made, especially in the areas of low-income housing and alternative fuels. "But going forward, our Number One goal will be to grow cash, which we will use to grow our business, buy back our stock and increase our dividends," he says. He notes that dividends have increased 20 percent a year since the company went public, despite ups and downs in the stock market and economy overall.

Chapter 20
Full Speed Ahead

"Skate to where the puck is going to, and not to where it's been."

Wayne Gretzky

The growth of Arthur J. Gallagher & Co. over the last 10 years has been phenomenal, and Gallagher's leaders believe that they have the understanding of their industry and the confidence in their company that will allow them to continue that growth. • "Our goal is to be $4 billion by 2012, and we'll do better than that," says Pat Gallagher. He notes that the company has strong stock, liquidity for acquisitions, extremely talented people, strong brokerage niches, growth in new areas like reinsurance, and a world-renowned franchise in Gallagher Bassett. • Pat estimates that the value of the entire insurance-selling marketplace in the United States could be as high as $100 billion, including commissions, fees and other revenues from selling insurance. "We're playing in a huge sandbox, and we only have about 1 percent of that now," he says. "If we don't make the big mistake, we're just getting started." • The company expects to grow by following the same strategy that it has always followed. "There was never, ever the option of not growing," says Pete Durkalski, vice president of operations support for the Brokerage Services Retail Division. Durkalski's job is to "coordinate and facilitate and oversee" the support functions for the company. He has developed operations standards and brought increased professionalism to the "back-room" functions of the company. It is a complex job because at AJGCo., each division develops its own strategy for growth, based on its goals and its strengths.

"That is important to the success of each division–going with your strengths," Durkalski says.

Durkalski joined AJGCo. in 1973 and, except for a brief stint with an e-commerce venture, he has been with it ever since. "We've always had a three-pronged attack," he says, including growing through acquisitions, through adding new talent and through the creation of new business by existing employees.

Mergers have been and will continue to be critical to Gallagher's growth. From December 1, 2000, to June 13, 2002, AJGCo. tied for 4th-most-acquisitive U.S. company, with 23 total acquisitions, according to TheDeal.com. But, unlike many of its competitors, Gallagher has been very selective in choosing its partners. "We are very cautious–and sometimes criticized as being too cautious– when we are finding merger partners," says Norm Darling, executive vice president and COO for Gallagher Bassett. "We don't buy broken shops."

Gallagher also is constantly on the lookout for talented people and for ways to grow new business. The recent producer hires and business expansions have helped to position the company to continue its exceptional growth. And, as it has throughout its history, the company relies on several unique strengths.

First, Gallagher's leaders have a clear idea of who they are and where they are going. From the start, they have understood that theirs is a sales company, and that they depend on providing superior products and services.

"Our identity is very, very strong," says Sam Babington, who heads the Mergers and Acquisitions Niche. "We're a production-oriented company. The old-fashioned broker is alive and well at Gallagher."

Craig Van der Voort, corporate vice president for market relations, believes the company will continue to grow because "we're always hungry. And we've always had a sales culture. We are a new business machine.

"As a company, we've never, ever been complacent or content with our position in the industry. No one's ever been bigger than the company," Van der Voort says.

Gallagher also benefits from a stable, strong, long-term management. There is very little turnover at the top. Pat jokes that most of the senior management has been together for 20 years or more. Meetings, he says, "are like siblings at the dinner table. Everyone knows his own seat."

John Stancik, head of Brokerage Services Retail's Northeast Region, recalls a meeting with a potential merger partner. He and two other Gallagher officers were at the meeting, and after a while, the merger partner said, "You guys sure seem to know a lot about this company." Stancik laughed and said, "We ought to–between the three of us, we have more than a hundred years here."

This stable leadership and established culture create an atmosphere in which even newcomers can adapt quickly. Doug Brown, area president in New York, joined Gallagher in April 2002, but he already understands the way things work. "The company has strong leadership, clear leadership, and it's accessible. They know what they want to do, they know what they want to be, and they stick to it," he says. "Ours is a sales culture. We say, 'Nothing happens until we sell something.'"

A stable, loyal management is mirrored in a stable, loyal employee base. Pat Gallagher believes that the company's culture empowers employees and encourages them to care strongly about the company and to personally commit to its growth. He notes that the success of the employee is tied literally and philosophically to the success of the company. Every year, the company distributes stock options to employees. The leadership of each division seeks recommendations for distributing the options, based on the prior year's contribution to the company's success. "They go all the way down to the mailroom," Pat says.

The stock options have a 10-year vesting, which is by design. The relatively long vesting period encourages people to commit to the company for the long term, and it also offers some protection from short-term fluctuation in the stock price. "It is a way of passing on a reward to people for our long-term success," Pat says. "And culturally, it continues to bind us."

In 2003, the company started an employee stock option purchase plan, and 20 percent of employees participated in the first year. Pat expects even more employees to take advantage of the plan as it moves forward. And, he believes, this will empower and connect them even more.

Employee loyalty and commitment are extremely important to the Gallagher culture. The company gives employees considerable freedom and encourages them to take a personal stake in the company's success. "This company is a steady grower because it allows individuals to be entrepreneurial and responsible," says CFO Doug Howell. "They allow the relationship and networking fabric to stay in place."

Gallagher's efforts to make employees feel connected to the company are working. The company recently conducted its first-ever employee survey, which garnered an exceptional 78 percent response rate. Overwhelmingly, employees were anxious to give their opinion of the company, and that opinion was overwhelmingly positive.

Almost all–96 percent–of respondents say they understand the need for Gallagher to grow and are committed to that growth. In addition, 92 percent say they are proud to work at Gallagher, and 90 percent say they are treated with respect by the people with whom they work. These are very impressive results, especially for a survey with anonymous responses.

The effort to build strong employees begins with a well-developed plan for hiring and training. When Gallagher managers talk about their employee family, sometimes they are speaking literally. The company is populated with family members, and its leaders see this as one of its strengths.

"We have a very successful track record of benevolent nepotism," Pat says. "We pick family trees clean." But he is quick to add that "with the policy of benevolent nepotism comes responsibility." People who do not fulfill their responsibilities at Gallagher, or who don't fit in with the culture, do not last long–no matter how they are related.

"I think the family connection is so important–it drives the culture," says Jennifer Gallagher, Pat's sister and the head of Innovative Risk Services. "It is so exciting to see us going into the fourth generation, and the talent pool in this group is incredible. The sense of family lends itself to a feeling of protectedness and support."

Many Gallagher people, including Pat Gallagher, are products of the company's well-respected Summer Internship Program. The program, which began in 1961 as The Manpower Program, offers employment to interested and qualified college students in the summer after their sophomore and junior years. It gives young people a taste of the business and of the company, and helps them decide if that is where they would like to start their professional lives. If both the intern and the company agree that the arrangement has worked, the intern is offered a job after graduation.

The intern program has grown considerably over the years, and now involves 80 to 100 summer interns. It also is being bolstered by the addition of Gallagher Scholars. These young men and women are part of a personal philanthropic effort of Bob Gallagher's to provide tuition assistance to deserving students in inner-city Catholic schools in Chicago. Gallagher Scholars who are interested in the business are now included in the Summer Internship Program.

The company also has instituted a new executive training program that targets young, "30-something" employees who might have management potential and brings them into the home office in Itasca for a weeklong training session. And it offers a wide variety of other training programs, many of them run by Gallagher employees who volunteer their time to help expand the knowledge of their colleagues.

In addition to finding and training the right people, Gallagher is preparing for the technological future–which is coming fast.

Technology played very little part in communication within the company before 1995–there were few personal computers, no e-mail, no networks. "We really had no need for it," says Nick Elsberg, Gallagher's chief information officer. Bob Gallagher Jr. was one of the first people in the company to use a personal computer, and his expertise earned him the nickname "Dr. Bob," as his colleagues called on him to help fix their computer problems.

Starting in 1995, the use of e-mail and networking became commonplace, and it fit right into the Gallagher culture of teamwork. One of the first uses of technology in the company was to develop literally hundreds of in-house data bases, most of them created by Bob Gallagher Jr. These data bases cover company information and news, as well as sales and marketing tools, documentation and policy manuals. Virtually every niche has its own data base of the company's expertise in that particular area. These data bases are designed to help Gallagher employees share information and requests for information or help. "It was really very easy for people to just broadcast a plea for help," Elsberg says.

At Gallagher, the move to technology has always been focused on helping the company serve its clients. "We try to make sure it doesn't get in the way of relationships," Elsberg says.

New technologies share the same focus. For example, Gallagher is in the process of introducing Gallagher Insight, an online data base for clients. It grew out of CoverageFirst.com, a data base for registering all the independent agents who do business with AJGCo. The success of CoverageFirst.com gave rise to the idea that the company could use the Internet to let retail clients view their data online. "You can get a lot of data without having to worry about office hours or whether you can get hold of someone," says Wally Bryce, area president in Tulsa, Oklahoma, who spearheaded the development of Gallagher Insight. "We're making data available 24/7."

Gallagher is on the forefront of change in other areas as well, including the issue of corporate governance. Corporate scandals such as the collapse of Enron Corp., which left many of its employees not only out of work but also holding retirement funds filled with now-worthless Enron stock, prompted an overwhelming call for greater accountability and integrity in the management of U.S. corporations. One of the targets of this call for accountability was corporate boards that were overweighted with insiders, offering potentially little resistance to corporate malfeasance.

Arthur J. Gallagher & Co. was one of the first in its industry to redraw its board of directors to remove virtually all insiders. Gallagher had a 12-member board made up of six directors from inside the company and six from outside. In January 2004, the company announced it was moving to a board that includes only two insiders: Bob Gallagher and Pat Gallagher.

"This reflects our continued commitment to transparency in our management and financial processes," Pat says. "It reconfirms our company's longstanding commitment to integrity."

At the same time, though, Pat and Bob realized that the opinions and input of the company's operating managers were invaluable. They formed an Executive Management Committee to retain that input. The Executive Management Committee members attend board meetings and act as the key operating advisory committee to the board. This allows the board to benefit from their experience and perspective, and it also gives the company's operating managers direct access to the thoughts and concerns of the board.

However, the members of the Executive Management Committee have no vote on the board. This maintains the "longstanding commitment to integrity" that characterizes Gallagher's approach to corporate governance.

Integrity and openness are cornerstones of the Gallagher culture. And it is that culture, company leaders believe, that directs and enables the company's growth.

"The culture is entrepreneurial, demanding, rewarding," says Bryce. "When push comes to shove, it's the most valuable asset in the company."

"I find this culture to be spectacular," says Howell. "It's a support environment of respect and safety, not a fear environment. You want to succeed for yourself, but also to improve the company."

It is a culture that focuses on client service. "Ours is the most incredible culture for a company this size," says Dave Marcus, vice president of the Southeast Region. "We all understand that whatever is best for the client in the long run will be best for Arthur J. Gallagher."

It is also a culture that offers respect and friendship. People who succeed in the company share many of the same values, and they genuinely like each other. "It's really hard to put into words the feeling of fellowship," says Dave McGurn, president of the Specialty Marketing and International Division. In his 25 years with the company, McGurn says, he has been continually impressed with the easy way in which even top management encourages the formation of friendships. "At the end of the day, we have fun together," he says.

Gallagher people routinely talk about a sense of family. Jim McFarlane, who heads the West Coast Region, says, "We settle our differences like a family. We are fiercely loyal to each other."

Like a family, they sometimes disagree, but they always come back to their shared goals. In the end, the people who make up the lifeblood of Arthur J. Gallagher & Co. believe that they are part of a very special culture. And they believe it is the reason for their continued success.

"The culture is everything," says Darling. "It's the heartbeat we all operate from....It's the thread that binds us together."

Central to that culture is an appreciation of the efforts of every employee, and that appreciation comes from the very top of the organization. Pat Gallagher says, "We're still learning, And a big part of our growth in the future will come from learning from each other.

"We're trying to go from good to better, and ultimately to best."

Leadership: Observations from a Lifetime

♦

by Bob Gallagher

1. Good leaders understand that family and health come before business.

2. The first thing leaders must be is true to themselves. Over time your skills can go up and down, so work on them.

3. The best leaders are visionaries.

4. True leaders are open, accessible, competitive and opportunistic.

5. Good leaders are loyal to their people and expect loyalty in return.

6. Leaders learn everything that is important in their industry. They become lifelong students of their trade. Continuing education is part of the job.

7. The best leaders are people persons.

8. Leaders have high activity levels.

9. Leaders of public companies know that real wealth is achieved by building shareholder values. Sharing equity with employees through stock participation plans accelerates this process.

10. Leaders are responsible for influencing the behavior of others.

11. Leaders have a passion to be the best.

12. Leaders focus on building a winning culture. They mold it and work at it. Culture is very important, and it can be a magnet for people and companies.

13. True leaders are students of people. Each individual has a different temperament, and handling this requires study, tact and knowledge. There is no one-size-fits-all in handling people.

14. The best leaders are moral and ethical.

15. Leadership requires courage.

16. Leaders are tough. Many decisions must be made, and some go against the beliefs of the majority. Leaders know that making the hard calls is not going to win them any popularity contest.

17. Leaders know that there is great power in listening. Often you can forget the words. What's the melody telling you?

18. The one thing leaders need is followers. People want to be led.

19. Leaders who treat people fairly build respect and more followers.

20. Leaders know good risk management. Thou shalt not make the big mistake. So don't make one.

21. Leaders understand themselves. They are objective, honest and open. Truth always wins in the end.

22. True leaders have their personal lives under control.

23. True leaders believe in God, know how to pray and do so often. Our company is divinely inspired. Many might call it luck, and a lot of that helps. The Irish are lucky.

24. Leaders have a need to help others.

25. Leaders drive out the curse of fear.

26. Good leaders study history and focus on the world and its varied cultures. We at Arthur J. Gallagher & Co. seek worldwide growth.

27. Leaders understand that price is what you pay, but quality is what you get. Quality lasts. A cheap price is a cheap thrill. It won't last.

28. Good leaders know that the client is king. They give clients what they want and need.

29. Empathy is a huge advantage in building leaders.

30. The best leaders are happy, upbeat, positive. No matter how dark the hour, they never show or express fear to others. As Ike once said, "If you want to cry, go home and cry in your pillow–but never in front of the troops."

31. Leaders know that a positive mental attitude is infectious. It wins and builds happiness throughout life.

32. The world, society and business are in constant change. Leaders change with it.

33. Leaders are creative and invent new things and ways to improve performance and results. They are at the cutting edge of change.

34. Good leaders keep their egos under control. Real power comes with respect, not the position.

35. Leaders should never do anything they wouldn't be proud to explain on national television.

36. Leaders should never ask someone to do something they wouldn't do themselves.

37. Leaders understand that if it's not in writing, it's not in this world.

38. Leaders know that all growth and progress come from profit.

39. Planning and execution are extremely important. Leaders involve others in leading the planning process. They make it a group mission. Real commitment comes from making it "their" idea.

40. Leaders should divide employees into A, B and C categories. A employees do a great job. Bs are good employees; they could move to A class or stay where they are. Either way, they're helping the organization. Cs just tread water. They don't work hard or do anything beyond what the job requires. They have a poor attitude, and they bitch and moan a lot. Leaders should get rid of their Cs. They hold you back.

41. The hardest job in the world is to fire someone, but it's part of business. Leaders should gather all of the facts and study past performance reviews. Be open, truthful and just, giving the person ample time to improve. Then implement the plan.

42. Leaders learn a lot from their mistakes. They make decisions fast. If it's the wrong decision, then re-do it. Telling the world, "I blew it!" when you did, builds followers.

43. Leaders recognize star players early. Move them up in the organization. Give them the jobs that best fit their talents and temperaments.

44. Leaders understand that the worst decision in the world is the one that's never made.

45. Leaders never, ever give up.

46. It's tough to balance career time and family time, but a balance must be achieved. A happy spouse and children come first.

47. Leaders should have fun. Laugh a lot. Be a participant in life.

48. The best leaders never close their office door. Being available takes discipline. An open-door society is better than a closed-door one.

49. Leaders should have a life plan. Be involved in community affairs or charitable work. Helping others is hugely satisfying.

50. A pat on the back costs nothing, and is most appreciated by the recipient. Leaders should never be stingy in this regard.

51. At the right time, leaders should use their wealth and talents to do something for others. Concentrating on accumulating toys is often destructive.

52. If money destroys a marriage or a person, then it hasn't been worth all the effort to achieve the wealth. Leaders must remember that family comes first.

January 2003

Growth History

✦

1995-2004

The Growth History at the end of Volume I shows Arthur J. Gallagher & Co.'s impressive growth from a small company to a major U.S. broker. This Growth History tells an even more dramatic story, of the company's explosive expansion to more than $1.5 billion in revenues and one of the top brokerage companies in the world.

Year	Gross Revenues	Net Earnings	Employees	Per Capita Revenues
1995	$411,998,000	$41,491,000	3,739	$110,189
1996	456,679,000	45,803,000	3,939	115,938
1997	488,028,000	53,316,000	4,000	122,007
1998	540,655,000	56,501,000	4,420	122,320
1999	605,836,000	67,753,000	4,755	127,410
2000	740,596,000	87,776,000	5,410	136,894
2001	910,043,000	125,256,000	6,488	140,266
2002	1,101,222,000	129,739,000	7,111	154,862
2003	1,304,500,000	146,200,000	7,206	181,030
2004	$1,521,600,000	$188,500,000	8,204	$185,000

About the Author

In the early 1990s, I began to think that it was time to write a corporate history of Arthur J. Gallagher & Co. I believed then, as I believe now, that we had a unique and compelling story to tell, and I wanted to get it on paper while many of the "old-timers" were still around to contribute their special perspectives.

I began looking for an author and, thankfully, I found Alison Kittrell. Alison is a respected journalist and business writer, with almost 30 years experience. She worked in daily journalism, including serving as copy desk chief when The Kansas Times won a Pulitzer Prize in 1981 for its coverage of the Hyatt Regency hotel disaster. She then moved to business journalism, becoming copy editor at Business Insurance magazine before co-founding her own company, Gaynor Communications.

Alison Kittrell is very familiar with the intricate world of risk management and insurance, and she is also intelligent, enthusiastic and a skilled interviewer. As such, she was the perfect candidate to piece together our long, interesting history.

We completed the first part of our corporate history in 1996. But only a scant eight years later, I knew we needed to update. Much had changed, especially our growth into a billion-dollar company and the third-largest brokerage in the United States. But much had stayed the same, especially our commitment to our clients and our culture. Alison was able to pick up where she had left off, and create a seamless work that outlines the full history of an extraordinary company.

Robert E. Gallagher
Chairman
2005

www.ingramcontent.com/pod-product-compliance
Lightning Source LLC
Chambersburg PA
CBHW030921180526
45163CB00002B/421